eselling®

eselling®

Sean McPheat

Matador
5 Weir Road
Kibworth Beauchamp
Leicester LE8 0LQ, UK
Tel: (+44) 116 279 2299
Fax: (+44) 116 279 2277
Email: books@troubador.co.uk
Web: www.troubador.co.uk/matador

ISBN 978 1848766 785

eselling® book cover image credit goes to ©iStockphoto.com/ Elena Genova

British Library Cataloguing in Publication Data.
A catalogue record for this book is available from the British Library.

Typeset in 11pt Verdana by Troubador Publishing Ltd, Leicester, UK
Printed and bound in the UK by TJ International, Padstow, Cornwall

Matador is an imprint of Troubador Publishing Ltd

I'd like to dedicate this book to my wife, Donna, for continually supporting me in all that I do and for putting up with all of my ideas over the years! I'd like to dedicate this book to my parents, Margaret and Barrie McPheat for always "being there" for me, to my in-laws Linda and John for all that they do and finally I'd like to thank my beautiful daughter Holly who always puts a smile on my face no matter what type of day I've had and who reminds me who I'm doing all of this for!

eselling®

The Obligatory Legal Stuff!

Table of Contents

Preface

Wow!

I honestly can't believe that you're reading this.

For someone like me who has the attention span of a gnat, to actually sit down and write a book is a miracle in itself!

It's been a long hard slog to get the book completed throughout the last 12 months. Not through the want of trying I hasten to add but because I've been very busy implementing and reaping the rewards of all that I'm about to cover with you in this book.

But I would say that wouldn't I?!

I could have written a sales book years ago. I've written enough material, tips and newsletters to fill several books! I've also been badgered and pestered to do so but I had always made my mind up that my first book would be "something different".

Now you're not going to find any sneaky sales tricks or "magic bullet" techniques in this book!

You're not going to find "455 ways to close the deal" and you're not going to find "267 ways to answer the price objection" either.

I mean, come on!

When I was going through the final editing process for the first ever print run of eselling® back in March 2011, I took time out and searched for "sales techniques" in the books department on Amazon.com. I was amazed to find that there were over 6,000 results for the term and "sales training" had over 2,500 results as well.

SEAN MCPHEAT

I mean, there's only so much to learn about the art and science of selling!

Now during the past couple of years we've trained and helped thousands and thousands of sales professionals. I've heard of the good, the bad and the damn right ugly of what they do and how they do it.

I've heard of, and seen first hand, the effort it takes to "get in the door" with a new prospect.

I've seen the way that our buyers have become more and more sales savvy and astute in the way that they negotiate with sales people, and with the economic downturn it's made selling that little bit more challenging!

So can anything be done differently to what's in all of those 6,000 sales books to even up the contest between the seller and the buyer?

And it is a buyer's market by the way. It always has been and always will be.

At the end of the day, people buy. And no matter how you try to "sell them", it's the prospect or your existing client who "buys" – they love to feel in control of the purchasing decision and they get turned off by sales tactics.

So during the past couple of years I've asked myself the question:

"Surely there's an easier way to prospect and sell than this?"

Over and over I've asked myself questions like:

What will the future of cold calling be like in 5 or 10 years' time?

How are sales professionals going to prospect if cold calling becomes less and less effective?

Is there an easier and better way to prospect and sell?

Researching and answering questions like those just threw up even more questions!

Questions like:

What will the role of the Internet play in the future of selling?

How do current buyers make their purchasing decisions?

Should sales professionals be using social media, Web 2.0 and all of that jazz?

What will the sales professionals role be like in 5 years' time?

You see, I needed to be crystal clear in my own mind about all of those issues before I put pen to paper.

The result of all of my thoughts, research and day-to-day trainings?

eselling®!

eselling® is all about using the Internet to position yourself as a trusted advisor so new business leads and your existing clients call and email you!

After all, that's the holy grail isn't it?

Prospects and clients who contact you are of a greater quality than all others!

Now let's just take a step back and be clear for a moment.

eselling® is not a replacement for traditional forms of prospecting

SEAN MCPHEAT

and selling, instead it's an addition to and an enhancement of what you are currently doing.

Many times you can combine the two.

It's also not just about social media and social networking either. Don't be confused about that.

eselling® is all about **USING THE INTERNET** to help you to:

- Network and prospect with key decision makers directly and to forge contacts within organisations who can get you to the key decision makers

- Listen out for potential new business leads

- Position yourself as a trusted advisor and expert within your industry

- Use different types of media like video, audio and whitepapers to set you apart from the rest

- Use social media and social networking in the right way without wasting your time!

- Prospect on the Internet

- Research about what your marketplace wants

- Research about what your competitors are doing

- Use your online status as an offline selling tool

- Be found when prospects are conducting research on available options

There are many others!

The bottom line is that by using the Internet effectively it will help your offline selling efforts and will enable you to close more deals because of the way you position yourself. You'll also create a personal brand that will encourage new prospects and your existing clients to call and email you.

I'm also showing you my hand too!

I can tell you that I use every single method and approach that you're going to discover within this book. I've made millions using them over the years and now you can too.

So let's get to it!

I wish you all the best in your selling efforts. Erhum, I mean eselling® efforts of course!

Sean

Introduction

If you're anything like most of the sales professionals that I've encountered over the past few years then you're in desperate need of a lifeline!

The economy has taken a massive beating, the type and usage of technology has seen a rapid increase and buyers seem to want more and more and want to pay less and less!

Of course, if you're long enough in the tooth then you've probably seen recessions come and go but that's not all that's going on here.

There's much more in play than the good old "economy excuse" of why you're not meeting your sales targets.

You see, the nature of relationships between sales people and customers has shifted. Your clients are busier than ever before. Calling them during business hours sets their teeth to a grind. There may be more ways than ever to contact someone, but that doesn't mean the attempts are always welcomed; they're typically viewed as interruptions.

The environment of selling has also changed – and is continuing to change – to a radical degree. The Internet has brought us the "Information Age" and has put unprecedented amounts of data and information at the fingertips of any person capable of forming a few searches through Google. With a few clicks of a mouse, you can look at pictures of cats wearing tutus, and retrieve information on the latest data management techniques for just in time inventory systems.

Ahhh, the beauty of the internet!

SEAN MCPHEAT

And no matter what industry you're in, you are no longer the gatekeeper for information about your products and services. Often, your clients and prospects will know as much as you do by the time that you've met. On top of that, your clients and prospects have checked up on you and have formed opinions of you based on whatever came up from the graces of the search engines. To the average web jockey, what they find, or don't find about you can make or break a sale.

eselling® is the lifeline that pulls you into the 21st century.

The Background To eselling®

Over the past couple of years, I've watched how the sales profession has been changed by the online world.

Changes in personal and corporate behaviours that would have taken years and decades to come about in the past are thundering into reality like a tornado.

Now while the fundamentals of selling remain the same, i.e. finding out what our prospect's wants are and then selling to those wants, the process of selling and more importantly the way that people buy has changed radically. And this change has come about because our prospects and clients are much more knowledgeable about the products and services that we sell, they are far more sales savvy than ever before and they have been sold to hundreds of times both online and offline.

As a sales professional, I've watched these same issues arise in my own businesses too.

More calls were required to get in touch with prospects and when we did speak with someone, they often seemed amazingly well-versed in our offering.

Where were they getting all this information from?

Conversations with colleagues and our existing clients revealed similar experiences. Clearly some major changes were happening. I had no intention of getting caught behind such a trend so I set out to get in front of the wave and master it.

The challenges being faced did not just stop with cold calling and prospecting.

When prospects were approaching businesses they seemed to know exactly what they wanted and how they wanted it. They had done their research beforehand and nearly had as much knowledge about the product or service as the sales person did!

Today's modern buyer is a different animal. And they are a different animal due to the Internet and the ready availability of the information and research that the Internet provides at the drop of a hat.

The model presented in this book is based upon a combination of my own trial and error efforts along with an intense study of the best practices required to readdress the balance of power with the modern day buyer.

I'm going to show how you too can use the Internet to get the upper hand in the sales interaction. And that's what eselling® is all about.

Like many sales professionals I looked at the Internet with some initial scepticism.

Sure it might be a good platform for driving consumer sales, but was such a platform really necessary for professionals in B2B settings?

As the Internet continued to mature, and as its users became more comfortable with the medium, it became quite evident that it was an

SEAN MCPHEAT

essential tool for any sales professional in any market. In a way, marketing, sales and PR have merged online to form a more personal conduit between buyers and sellers.

I believe this truth is driven by one essential fact. No matter what you're selling, people are part of the equation. People love to feel in control of the sales process and those people are using the Internet to look up information about products and solutions because they expect to find everything online. Whoever provides that information has a big advantage over the other guy who is knocking on doors and making calls with sales data sheets in hand.

Sales meetings are no longer the vehicle for the discovery of solutions. Your client already googled that information during his or her lunch break or after the kids went to bed.

In this book, you'll learn how to use the eselling® model to close more sales. It's how you build strong customer loyalty and trust. eselling® confirms your authority and competence online. Being an authority doesn't just mean that you know your stuff.

Through the tested strategies covered in this book, you can deliver needed value to your clients and prospects any time of the day or night. People you've never met before may be introduced to you first through your online presence. That presence then leads them to you as the sales process continues.

Authority also conveys trust in you as a guide. Your clients and prospects will see you as a solutions partner and someone who can bundle together the limitless myriad of information online and present it in terms that speak directly to their needs.

Keep in mind that even though eselling® involves activities on the Internet, the online world is still the "real" world. People reading your profile on LinkedIn, watching videos on YouTube or reading your blog are real people. Being online makes them no less real so throw any perceptions of virtual vs real world out of the window. People are people and the Internet is just a tool that connects you with them.

If you can type on a keyboard, address an email and surf the web, you have the requisite skills to build your online presence. The tools covered were designed to be used not by an elite few but by tens of millions of people.

Online services like blogging, Facebook, YouTube and LinkedIn were designed to be used by you and the people with whom you network.

As you read about eselling® in this book, keep in mind that it is presented as a framework and a model for connecting with your customers – current and future – through a number of different avenues online.

I'm not going to tell you how to carry out sales transactions or how to communicate in terms and styles best understood by your target audience. That's something you must bring to the table. As a sales professional, you're an essential element in that equation and that can't be replaced by any set of processes.

So use this book as a roadmap as well as a guidebook for your efforts to build a strong presence online.
Don't wait until all the planets are in perfect alignment before getting started!

Instead, pick one of the strategies or approaches that you're going to cover and then get started.

As you get the hang of one approach, add another. Mastery comes with practice, not endless contemplation!

SEAN MCPHEAT

The Challenging World Of Sales Today

Today, we have a world population of about 6 billion people. The Internet and cheap phone calls make it easier to connect – technologically speaking – than ever before. Advances in information technology, service delivery and manufacturing make it possible to build products and services that suit almost anyone.

So why then, does it seem that the actual process of finding people who want to buy your goods and services has become so difficult when it's obvious that those people are out there?

You see, in today's world of sales just about everything has become that little bit more difficult. It seems that the problem is not one of supply and demand but rather a growing rift between how people want to buy and how some sales people continue to sell.

It's long been said that people hate to be sold to but they love to buy. This is true even in murky economic times. Just look at the sales for Plasma TVs and other consumer items like smart phones, tablet PCs, online music, broadband Internet connections and hybrid cars. It's hard to describe how anyone would need any of these products and yet the sales of these items are strong and even record-breaking.

So what's the problem?

It's easy to say that things have changed, but how have they changed? Are people really all that different? Has human psychology changed so much that we're almost dealing with a new race of beings?

Fortunately, the fundamentals of what makes up the psyche of a

eselling®

person and population haven't really changed all that much. Instead, what has changed is how we're able to interact, how often those interactions occur and how we're able to use an unprecedented level of access to information to protect our own minds from a deluge of attempts to get our attention from the outside world.

This has led to changes in the way that we make our purchasing decisions. To better understand these changes, challenges, and trends, it's valuable to look at the profession of sales and influence along a timeline.

Selling In The Past

Go back far enough in time and you will find sales as an active profession!

After all, what is sales?

It's all about connecting people with what they want or need. Jokes aside about the oldest profession in human history, sales really is the oldest profession in the book! That second-oldest profession wouldn't have been possible unless the proprietor was engaging in sales.

There weren't nearly as many people walking the earth then as there are today.

You could literally walk for weeks before seeing any signs of other human life. At a bazaar, what was available for sale?

There were fruits, meats, water skins and other provisions you could probably identify with ease. After haggling over a price, you exchanged your money for a measure of "stuff" and went on your way. And if a merchant was a dishonest cheat, you stabbed him with a spear!

The Show Up And Throw Up Era

Fast forward to the not-so-distant past and things look a little different.

Manufactured goods have entered the scene and it's not so obvious what makes one product good and another product bad. Sometimes something might look shiny and life-altering in the showroom but falls apart the moment it's put into service. Industrial products could be even more complicated. As a buyer, how are you supposed to know how much horse power your plant needs to turn out widgets? In these settings, sales professionals were also consultants who helped you figure out what you needed. You trusted them to deliver.

With the advent of the telephone, motorised transportation, reliable mail delivery and even the emerging forms of mass media, it was now possible to find people to buy your stuff instead of waiting for them to walk by. There was once a time when picking up the phone was like waving a magic wand. "Dialling for dollars" some called it. People almost marvelled that you were calling them to offer a product or service. Few people were ever too busy to talk to a sales person about something they might need.

How times have changed! Lead generation at public gatherings and networking events was often successful.

At a networking event, handing out your business card was an easy way to get a call back. Other sales people would actually trade leads with you and even make referrals based upon the impression that you left on them from only a brief encounter. An hour at a networking event was well worth the time and was a great way to build your reputation as an expert in your field.

Back then, buyers were less savvy about their purchasing decisions.

Often they had to trust the sales person to steer them in the right direction, and usually sent out signals indicating they knew virtually nothing about the product they were trying to buy. People would literally kick the tyres of a new car – an indicator of absolutely nothing – and expected the sales person to tell them what the best product was, and to help them make the final purchase decision.

That didn't mean people were dumb. Rather, that you as the sales person had a level of knowledge about your products that was almost always greater than that of your prospects and customers. After all, where would they go to learn about your product but to your showroom?

Advertising was much more effective in the past too.

Remember that big book with the really thin paper pages? That's the phone book you know!

Not too many years ago, an ad in the phone book was almost guaranteed to make your phone ring, unless the ad was really, really bad. Radio and TV advertising worked well too. Ads were actually listened to and/or seen.

Direct mail was also a great way to generate leads and sales as well. A good long-copy sales letter could generate guaranteed income for years running.

In fact, taking a walk down the street and knocking on doors was a highly successful technique for bringing in sales.

All it took was guts and persistence.

It should come as no surprise that this era is what I call as **"The Show Up and Throw Up Era"**.

SEAN MCPHEAT

The Show Up & Throw Up Era

SALES PERSON   **PROSPECT**

The dialogue was all one way!

All it took to be successful in sales was the guts to knock on enough doors or make enough phone calls and to be persistent until the sale was made.

Many of the "tried and untrue" sales tactics people think of when imagining the stereotypical sales person derive from this era.

They were intended to wear down the defences of the prospect until they either bought or threw you out!

How times have changed...

eselling®

The Consultative Selling Revolution

As people began to become more wary of the old sales processes and tactics, some began to move into a more consultative role.

This put more emphasis on a two-way dialogue between sales person and the prospect. Some began to think of customers more as clients, which comes from a word meaning a person who is under the care and protection of another.

A client-oriented sale is more collaborative and focused on the needs of the client rather than the quota of the sales person.

Consultative selling was a major advancement and should still be used as a basis for selling but, until the advent of the Internet, the buyer was still largely at the mercy of the sales person for accurate information about their products and services and how they could solve their problems and fulfil their needs.

In many cases, the sales person would literally write an RFP (request for proposal) for the client to hand back to the sales person.

The RFP would also be forwarded to the competition, but the one writing the RFP on behalf of the client always seemed to have the product solution which offered a perfect fit to the list of requirements.

Selling In Today's World

Today, it's harder to generate leads and to qualify prospects.

Cold calling today requires many unsuccessful calls simply to generate a lead. The process also leaves you in a poor position with the person you're calling.

When you call someone in this way, you're seen in the context of a stereotype.

The person on the other end of the line sees you as the desperate sales person.

Even though placing a phone call has become very inexpensive, the time required to put food on your table by cold calling has made this approach to sales a real challenge.

Networking is a time-consuming process that generates less in sales than the time required to make it work and we all like to avoid lengthy traffic queues and hold-ups on the motorway! These gatherings tend to involve meeting groups made up of other sales people looking for their own leads. It's like watching an underfed koi pond. The first sign of a morsel brings everyone running like zombies at the first smell of

brains. The last thing on their mind is to buy something from you.
Not unlike cold calling, networking tends to generate few long-term, beneficial effects. The next meeting you show up to often results in the same blank stares as you make your way around the room, shaking hands.

Word-of-mouth advertising and selling still does occur but most of the activity has shifted to the Internet. In fact to expect even verbal referrals from friends and clients, you need to have an active online presence as anyone who hears of you is most certain to use Google, or one of the other major search engines, to look you up and learn more about you before even thinking about placing a call, sending an email or completing an order online.

The Start Of The Research Age

The power of word-of-mouth selling on the Internet has become like a force of nature and most of the time it's not easy to control.

This is the start of the research age where people seek out information on their own terms.

Instead of dealing with the interruptions of standard sales and marketing tactics, people may be doing their own research at 2.00 a.m.

These people aren't just accepting the information as presented by others either.

They might be forming their own lists of resources using social media bookmarking for example.

Some may keep a blog or share documents using free services from the likes of Google. All of this content adds to what was already there.

Start Of The Research Age

SALES PERSON

PROSPECT

Online, the masses control the message, making the results of the Internet like word of mouth on steroids. Some may love your product, and some may hate it. Few are afraid to share their opinions in the full view of the World Wide Web.

Movies have seen their box office sales plummet from Friday to Saturday due to online social media traffic slating the film while others have had their box office numbers raised beyond expectations due to viral messages on the Internet. In some cases, people have used Twitter, while still at the theatre watching the movie, to tell the world how much they love or loathe it!

For example, if you planned to see the movie Inception, you might make a quick search through Twitter to see what other people are saying. Even weeks after the release of this film, positive chatter is easily found.

 was fantastic. Never have I thought about a movie so deeply and yet had so many "a-ha!" moments. Incredible film.
less than a minute ago via web

 Saw MIND = BLOWN. Exceeded all my expectations!
2 minutes ago via txt

 THE BEST movie of the year
2 minutes ago via Twee

In one famous example of the message being controlled by the masses, the Internet news site Digg received a post from a user one day. It was a string of numbers. To the technologically savvy it was the sequence necessary to decrypt the digital data on DVDs!

Within hours, thousands of people had "Dugg" this story, which essentially votes it as a top story. By the time the movie industry responded with threats from lawyers, the message had been reposted to thousands of blogs and had been reported upon by other media outlets.

Removing this message from the Internet would have been utterly impossible and the attempts by the movie industry lawyers to squelch the information was like pouring gas on a fire and caused the story to spread even further and faster than it might have if left alone.

More on this subject later, but know this: **your online presence is what eselling® is all about.**

It's all about building up your expert status online so prospects and clients hunt you out. It's all about building up a persona that you can use both online and offline to take you to that coveted "trusted advisor" status. It's about having a deep understanding of the problems, the challenges and the gossip within your industry and using this to "listen in" to conversations and for possible further business opportunities.

It's about e-networking and prospecting online, engaging potential clients either directly or indirectly through others.

It's about building up your personal brand so that when you're competing for business, your credentials and brand trumps all others, it's about deepening the relationships that you have with your existing clients and it's all about networking online, prospecting and making fruitful friendships and connections that lead to bigger things!

Today's buyers are savvier when it comes to information about your products and services. They might even know more than you do too!

Seriously, I've seen this happen a lot when the buyer comes armed with reviews, statistics, Internet printouts – you name it!

Recent polls show that 1 in 5 in the UK and 1 in 4 in the US check online for reviews and information about products before making a purchasing decision.

By using the Internet to shop for bargains and do research before purchasing, the buyers have changed the balance of power in the sales process. This new activity doesn't mean that you have no value in the process, but you're no longer seen as the oracle, by default, as you once may have been.

Interestingly enough, price competition is not the strict motivator in sales decisions. As the saying goes, people like to do business with those they know, like and trust. People still buy premium, brand named items.

eselling®

Don't believe me?

Well, just take a look outside in the car park for all of the makes and models of the cars! Who said that all you need a car for was to get from A to B?!

To sell to the modern day buyer you need to position yourself online (your personal brand, products, company, etc.) to be seen as the authority and expert guide to purchasing decisions in your market niche, and all of this can be achieved through eselling®

To achieve this, your activities must focus around the generation of content online. This isn't done through a piecemeal approach but rather as a consistent strategy that builds upon itself. Your content is shared through different forms of online media. These broadly cover the forms of blogs, news releases, audio and video content, forum participation and social media sites like Facebook and Twitter.

Keep in mind though that while the technology of the Internet represents a rapidly growing movement and a massive paradigm shift in the way people are empowered to connect with each other, eselling® is about taking advantage of this movement, as a whole, but isn't tied to any particular website or service to work.

If YouTube, one of the highest traffic sites on the Internet today, vanished tomorrow, it wouldn't matter. Life goes on. Something will take its place. The paradigm of eselling® will continue.

Here's a brief summary of the kinds of online venues you can use to build your presence and authority online.

Blogs

A blog is a bit like an online journal or diary but offers so much more in terms of capabilities when it comes to connecting with your audience. The opportunity with a blog isn't just about being able to present you, what you know, and how you can help others. The ability to get feedback and connect directly with your reader gives you an amazing ability to check the pulse of the public.

Car maker General Motors created a blog that gets 100s of comments with every post. Some of the comments are very supportive, and others not so. The executives at GM understand that allowing such open feedback means they don't need to worry about trade magazine and car shows to talk directly to their customers.

The post below is a simple report of sales numbers and received 36 comments from the public. Notice the writing style from the Sales Vice President. He isn't writing in the third person but instead takes a very personal and authentic tone.

GM *FastLane Blog*   Photo of the Day   FYI   The LAB   Search this site

Sales Reflect Continued Growth in May

By Steve Carlisle
Vice President, U.S. Sales

I'm pleased to announce strong May sales for our four brands, which continued to grow at a double digit pace this month. Sales for Chevrolet, Buick, GMC and Cadillac increased 32 percent over May 2009, and we've delivered our eighth consecutive month of year-over-year sales gains.

GM's brands have outperformed the market this year on the strength of the company's newest products. Year-to-date, combined sales of the Chevrolet Equinox, Chevrolet Camaro, Buick LaCrosse, GMC Terrain and Cadillac SRX are up nearly 323 percent.

Chevy retail sales were up 19 percent in May, Buick retail sales rose 46 percent, GMC retail sales increased 37 percent, and Cadillac retail sales were up 43 percent.

Each of our brands has new products that are being received well by customers who are looking for style,

eselling®

This is a key factor in writing a successful blog. Write to your reader.

You need to run your own blog and use it to engage your market. Blogging isn't just about selling. It's about positioning yourself as a thought leader who thinks beyond the sale.

And when you add a new prospect in your sales funnel, you can direct them to these posts to help them in some way and at the same time you are building your brand.

Effective blogging also entails commenting on other related blogs too.

Thoughtful comments also help you to position yourself as someone to take notice of and because you normally have to leave a website address on the comment it also provides a trail back to your site. For those visitors who are impressed with your comments, they will most likely click on the link to your site for a further snoop around.

Richard Branson has a blog with his musings and ideas. Notice how simple it is.

The content is really what matters when it comes to a blog.

A common mistake made by companies is to invest more time in the look and feel of a blog than on the content itself. A clean and simple design draws the focus to what you have to say and not to the amazing talents of your graphic design team.

Good content will always keep people coming back for more.

Best-selling author Seth Godin also has a blog.

Not only does it have a very simple layout, characteristic of most successful blogs, but the individual posts are very short.

Sometimes a blog post on his site is a mere 200 words. The content is thought- provoking and intended to start a conversation.

You may think that a successful blog requires you to already be a large car company, a famous billionaire, or a best-selling author. Fortunately this isn't the case.

In the example of Seth Godin, he was blogging long before he became the well-known celebrity that he is today. By consistently engaging a growing audience through his blog, he developed a platform which made it easy to promote his books. People were coming to his blog to hear what he had to say and his books simply fed that need and provided an additional monetary benefit for Seth.

Encouraging feedback from your readers helps to ensure candid and honest remarks. This is better than any marketing focus group. You will find that brutal honesty will come as long as you create the environment for it. All of this means your company is better able to build what the market actually wants and you will be better equipped to speak to the needs of the customer and prospects you have.

(click on my head)

seth godin's
BLOG

DON'T MISS A THING

How long before you run out of talking points?

Here's how you know if someone is living the brand, is emotionally connected to the story and is literate and informed--or if they're just emotionally connected in the moment:

Ask a lot of questions.

Cornel West can talk for hours about race, the Bible or Marx. *He knows it cold.*

Dan Dennett can write for three hundred pages about the philosophy of free will and consciousness and he's just getting started. There's depth there.

I've talked to brand stewards from JetBlue and Starbucks that could go deep or wide or detailed for hours.

Then compare these passionate leaders to a pundit, spin doctor or troll (for just about any cause du jour) being interviewed on TV. After three sentences, they

In addition to your own blog, seek out other blogs on topics in your field or other blogs that are read by your ideal prospects.

Contact the blog owner and offer to write content as a guest blogger. Most bloggers are savvy enough to welcome guest content for their blog. It makes their own blog appear more of an authority and it almost instantly positions you as an authority by appearing on someone else's blog.

In exchange for your content, you'll end up with your profile, and a link to your blog, on the blog you're writing for. You're a virtual guest speaker with an arrow pointing back to your home base.

From my own blog at http://www.mtdsalesblog.com you can see how I use it to share ideas and let the public know more about who I am and what I stand for.

You, and any visitor, can see clearly across the top how to learn more about it, gain access to my products and services and even find suggestions and offers for "introductory material" in the form of reports I've written to help others learn more about the sales training my company offers.

SEAN MCPHEAT

The eselling® Mindset For Using Blogs

Just imagine that you sell photocopiers into businesses – surely there's no need to write a blog?

Well, you'd be wrong!

Here's what you could do to really stand out from the pack:

You could start a video blog that showcases different photocopier machines and you could review each one "LIVE". This raises you above a mere "salesperson" status and into the "expert" category. You could make sure that your existing clients receive each update so this keeps you in contact with them regularly and you can direct any of your prospects to the site to review some machines that they are interested in or the ones that they are most suited to.

eselling®

With this approach you are helping them to buy.

Then, you could think about where your prospects and potential clients "hang out" on the Internet.

These decision makers might be part of a group on LinkedIn or read business blogs or forums for example, so why not approach these resources and offer to write them a blog post or shoot a video that covers "How To Reduce Your Printing and Copier Costs In The Recession By 20%"

This is a very topical subject and blog owners are just crying out for content!

All of a sudden you've got in front of 50,000 potential new clients! And you're not selling a thing, you are educating them and helping them to become more successful.

And that's not all!

At the end of the blog/video you could direct the viewer back to your own blog to receive a freebie and then they can check out all of your other videos and content and you can innovatively get them on your emailing prospect lists etc. (but more on that later!).

I've just quickly illustrated the thinking that is required for the eselling® approach and that is just with the use of one source!

News

The world of news has changed drastically over the past few years. News releases used to require expensive effort to produce and distribute. After your news was released, there was no guarantee that any reporter would even be interested in what you had to say. If a media outlet didn't publish your story, no one else would hear anything about it. There was also a limit to how often you could, or should, put out news releases about yourself or your company. If reporters saw your name too often on the fax machine, they'd basically blacklist you and ignore everything from you.

Today, this has been turned on its head.

Not only can you distribute your news release for a fraction of what it used to cost, but you can include multimedia and also optimise your wording to be found through major search engines like Google.

News aggregation services like news.google.com will publish your news directly.

It doesn't matter if no one reports on your news because you'll still have direct access to the tens of millions of people who read their news directly through portals like Google and Yahoo every day. There are also no real limits to how often you can release fresh news about yourself. There's so much going on that few people would think anything negative if you put out a new piece of news every day for a year. There's a chance that few would see every one of those releases each day anyway, so doing so would only increase your chances of being seen by the right people.

As you build your presence with news releases, your authority online builds at the same time.

The average person neither knows, nor cares, how easy it may be to distribute news releases on the Internet today.

Your news release sends a message that you are for real and that you have something to say.

Video

For a very small investment, you can make your own videos and share them through online services such as YouTube for free.

You can create videos to educate your prospects and clients about your products and services; you can put together reviews of products and services in your marketplace, or even demonstrate how to use your products.

You can also review and comment upon the news in your industry. These activities give you a "real face" and help to develop trust and a sense of personal relationship with the viewer. Also, commenting upon the news in your industry positions you as a "thought leader" automatically.

Why is this?

Well, that's simple.

It's because no one else is doing it. So you become a thought leader by default!

When making your videos, let your real personality show through. Don't try to put on a front or a facade. Doing so is detectable by the viewer and also runs the risk of you building a following with people who are attracted to your act and not the real you.

Video content can be drawn from a variety of sources. If you've been on TV or the stage, you can slice these videos up into online clips. Using inexpensive camera equipment and lighting you can shoot live video from your office desk or from the showroom floor. You can also make your own "show me" style videos to present slide shows or PowerPoint presentations as the video content while you speak. There are many utilities for creating videos with your presentations including Camtasia, Screenflow, JingProject.com and SlideShare.net. As with live video, these videos can be shared through YouTube and other video sharing sites.

Another popular option for video is through websites like Ustream.tv and Justin.tv. With a simple webcam you can run a live broadcast and interact with your audience in real time.

Sessions can be recorded for on demand playback and can be used for product demonstrations, company announcements or simple chats while standing in front of a whiteboard.

Video editing is possible using free software available on any PC or Mac sold in the past 5 years.

If you're not technologically savvy enough to edit your own videos – or if you don't have the time – chances are the teenager next door can do it for a few quid!

The use of video shouldn't just be confined to blogs and content online either, you can use them with your offline selling efforts too.

Here's how...

The eselling® Mindset For Using Video

Imagine a prospect has approached your company. (Let's call him Steve Morgan.)

You have spoken to him on the phone and have arranged a meeting. (Let's call you Dave Hill and you work for a company called MW9 Printers.)

Now put yourself in the shoes of Steve for a moment ….

You've just put the phone down and are carrying on with your work. You might even be calling a competitor about the very same product or service.

Now 15 minutes later an email arrives in your inbox with the subject line "Hi Steve, here's our meeting confirmation".

When you open up the email, it says something like this:

Hi Steve,

Thanks for your call.

I've left a quick message for you below, please click on the link:

http://www.mw9printers.com/stevemorgan

Thanks again Steve

Dave

Now research shows that the most important words in the world are someone's name so Steve is going to click on that link just out of curiosity never mind anything else!

And what does Steve find?

Well, he finds a personal video of you thanking him for the call, confirming the date, location and time of the meeting and what the purpose of the meeting will be and what to expect.

WOW!

And that's not all, at the end of the video and also underneath the video itself is a link to Dave's blog where he's showcasing the latest copier machines. And there are links to where he's been distributing content on the web, including some of the major players in business blogs. There's also a link to 2 newspaper articles that Dave wrote in the business sections.

Now that's pre-meeting positioning!

So before Dave has even met with Steve he's already raised himself above that of a salesperson and into the expert status. Dave will command more respect, he'll be listened to more attentively and will be viewed as a trusted source rather than someone who is out for a commission.

Does it take extra effort to do all of this?

Damn right it does.

eselling®

That's why you can guarantee that the majority of sales people will not do it which gives you a competitive advantage.

And so what if it takes you an additional 30 minutes?

If it increases your closing ratios by 20% then it's all worth it!

But don't forget too that you could produce a standard greeting informing your prospect a little bit about yourself, who you've helped and what you do. With this, you have done the work once!

Podcasts

A podcast is like a radio show that has been pre-recorded and can be replayed at any time on- or offline.

People can play podcasts through their iPods, MP3 players and on their desktop and laptop computers. Some podcasts have picked up corporate sponsors from the likes of Ford Motors, Audible.com and Go2Meeting.

Originally named in relation to one of the most popular MP3 players of all time, the iPod, podcasts are supported by virtually any device and are even catalogued by multiple online services including iTunes, and podbean.com.

Like a video, a podcast gives you an opportunity to add a sense of connection with your audience. In other words, it makes you seem more real.

As a variation on the podcast, you can also run a live audio programme for free with the web-based service BlogTalkRadio.com. Shows made through this site can be recorded and redistributed as podcasts as well.

SEAN MCPHEAT

The trick to running a successful podcast is to treat it as a narrow themed talk radio show. Bring your personality into the programme and set out to entertain as well as inform. Podcasts can be of any length. One very popular podcast is about 90 seconds per episode and is on the topic of proper grammar in writing!!

Forums

Forums and "question and answer" areas give you the ability to position yourself as an authority and to get the pulse of your market by engaging others in conversation directly.

The business networking site LinkedIn.com provides an area for questions and answers on a limitless variety of topics. By answering questions, and by asking them, you position yourself and show your expertise and interests.

If you go to Google and enter a word describing your market and the word "forum" into the search box, you can probably find existing chat rooms and forums already set up where you can join active conversations about your industry.

Listen and participate to add to your online authority as well as gain valuable market insight about what people want.

For example, a search for "gardening forum" in Google revealed several forums where people actively discuss a broad range of related topics. These community sites are an amazing place to "check the pulse" of a market because these people are here because of a common interest.

They talk about the products they use and the challenges they have. Very little is held back in these forums making them an ideal place to meet up with end users and people of influence.

While not every industry may have a forum dedicated to its discussion, you may be surprised to find that your market is represented if you're thoughtful enough in your searches.

Social Media

If the entire Internet is a universe, then social media represents thousands of galaxies.

It has become the meat and potatoes of the Internet experience today. If you think that social media is only where teens hangout online then you are sadly mistaken. All age groups are represented on social media and these people are spending the majority of their time online using social media.

Social media is also known as Web 2.0 because of how it represents a huge shift in the way people use the Internet and by the fact that the masses are now largely in control of what happens online.

In the days of Web 1.0, websites were static, usually created by people with enough technical skill or fortitude to get a server running and create the pages necessary to display on your computer browser.

It was a broadcast medium where a few people controlled the message received by the many. Today, the many control the messages. One, or a few people, may create a video and upload it to YouTube, but the masses get to rate it, leave comments about it, refer to it from their own social media accounts and even embed the video in blogs and other web pages.

Messages and content can be repeated and shared so quickly online that news online can spread faster than the professional media outlets can broadcast it.

Recent evidence of this includes news of the earthquake in Haiti being reported from people in Haiti through Twitter and Iranian women reporting on the local elections from their mobile phones.

Social media is represented on major news media websites where people can offer comments on stories. Video sharing sites, like YouTube, allow people to comment and even to record video responses to videos. While these may seem like simple applications of the media, this simplicity is what drives the usage.

It is clear that the public is no longer satisfied by being a mere spectator of the world. They want to be a part of the story, as it happens. This ability to rapidly explore topics and to engage each other through the amazing reach of the World Wide Web has exposed corporate scandals, and even put long shot candidates into office.

Of the myriad of options available to engage others through the Internet, few exemplify the rapid nature of people engaging each other, worldwide, than Twitter.

Using ad hoc keywords known as "hash tags", conversations can be created and tracked on a variety of subjects.

For example, every Sunday evening people around the world come together for the informal "blogchat" to discuss issues around the world of blogging and media.

Here are some amazing statistics collected by econsultancy.com.

They should give you an idea of just how vast the landscape is when it comes to social media use on the Internet today.

These were compiled from various sources at the end of 2010.

- Facebook claims that 50% of active users log into the site each day. This means at least 250 million users every 24 hours

- Twitter had 150 million user accounts

- LinkedIn had over 100 million members worldwide

- Facebook had in excess of 500 million active users on global basis

- Flickr hosted more than 5 billion images

- Wikipedia had in excess of 14 million articles

- People spent an average of 700 billion minutes per month on Facebook

- There were more than 70 translations available on Facebook

- The average user had 130 friends within Facebook

- Mobile was even bigger than before for Facebook, with more than 200 million users accessing the site through mobile-based devices

- There were more than 30 billion pieces of content (web links, news stories, blog posts, etc.) shared each month on Facebook

- There were 5 million LinkedIn users across the UK

- Towards the end of 2010, the average number of tweets per day was over 90 million

- 46% of active users used some sort of mobile Twitter experience.

- More than 700,000 local businesses had active pages on Facebook

- The average Facebook user created 90 peices of content each month

- 15% of bloggers spent 10 or more hours each week blogging, according to Technorati's new State of the Blogosphere

- The average time spent on LinkedIn in the UK was 7.3 minutes.

- About 70% of Facebook users were outside the USA

- On the 4th Jan 2011 498,000 people from the UK visited LinkedIn – a record.

- People on Facebook installed 20 million applications each day.

- 70% of bloggers were organically talking about brands on their blog

- 38% of bloggers posted brand or product reviews.

Since social plugins launched in April 2010 an average of 10,000 new websites integrate with Facebook every day.

If there is a mistake to be made when it comes to social media, it is this: social media cannot be encapsulated into a single site or "example."

Social media is represented by an entire landscape that has shaped the entire Internet. It is characterised by the ability to bring people together interactively and will likely take future forms which no one has yet begun to imagine.

And you will be using social media and networking sites like LinkedIn, Facebook and Twitter to help you to build your brand as well as to network online with prospective clients.

The Long Tail

Another amazing and most interesting of trends that we're seeing in the world of selling right now is something called "the long tail".

"The Long Tail" was written about by Chris Anderson in his best-selling book and I highly recommend that you get yourself a copy if you haven't already done so.

So what exactly is the Long Tail?

Developed by Wired Magazine editor Chris Anderson in his 2006 book entitled "The Long Tail: Why the Future of Business is Selling Less of More," he refers to a graph showing fewer products selling in large quantities versus many more products that sell in low quantities.

When the traditional limitations of distribution and shelf space are

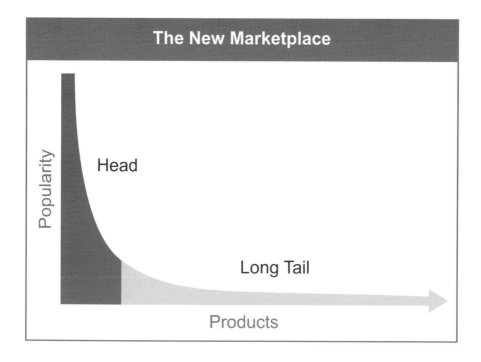

eliminated, or managed better through modern information technology, it turns out that people's interests are more varied than ever believed before.

Give people 2 million songs through Apple's iTunes and do you see the same narrow band of purchase variations seen in old record stores?

You see the opposite.

People dig deep through the libraries and purchase new music and old. They connect with bands and artists that may have otherwise never found any following. The long tail effect can show up in some unexpected ways.

With the introduction of the iMac, Apple changed the rules of buying a computer to a colour decision. With proper inventory tracking and management, they ran little risk of being stuck with too many of an unpopular colour.

Other computer manufacturers were dumbfounded as they continued to push features that a large group of the buying public had no interest in.

This effect is even seen in the supermarkets. Instead of the simple bag of white sugar, you'll find that some may carry five, ten or two dozen variations on the shelf. The long tail effect, plus incredible access to information online gives us the ability to be connoisseurs of anything that strikes our fancy.

This isn't to say that choice always leads to more sales.

Poorly managed or presented and too many choices can lead to confusion.

Confusion leads to fewer purchasing decisions. Too many choices can also carve up your delivery model so much that you can't deliver in a cost-effective manner.

Through the creation of educational content online, you can talk to your market about what interests them. You can also talk to them about what they are uninterested in as well. You can create a new market segment merely by talking about it through your blog, videos and status updates.

Becoming No.1 in Google for a short tail keyword like "Photocopier" is nearly impossible but a blog post with a long tail keyword like "Photocopier Options For Small Businesses" will give you a better chance of a high Google ranking although the demand for that keyword may be very low. But the approach here is to have hundreds of long tail keyword blog posts receiving 1 hit per day each rather than going for the unobtainable.

The 100 blog posts increases what I call your Internet footprint and the chances of someone interested in your products and services stumbling over your website.

The Future Of Selling

Today, while many of the traditional prospecting tools and approaches may still work in some settings, I think we're seeing the results from methods such as cold calling, direct mail and mass media advertising drop off so sharply they may become relics in the years to come.

Some of our younger generations report through interviews and polls that they would almost prefer to have mobile phones that don't include voice services!

They consider it an inefficient and outdated form of communication. How do you call leads that don't answer a call from their own friends?

Can you imagine what a sales text message might look like?

Do you want to buy? y/n

That's just ridiculous! But not completely out of the question.

Imagine in the future; you might be able to sign up to some supermarket programme where every Friday you receive a text message like this:

Would you like us to send you the same shopping that you purchased last week? y/n

You press y and then your shopping gets delivered automatically!

This would be great for ordering those weekly essentials that you couldn't go without.

But I digress!

Current attempts at business 2 business marketing and selling through text messaging have proven largely inconclusive and the traditional phone is most likely a dead end for sales professionals in the future.

I predict that cold calling may even be banned in the future due to invasion of privacy laws. After all, we're becoming a world where privacy rules! The fact that information is so readily available is a big win for the eselling® approach.

People will continue to use search engines to research information and people. People will prefer to network online rather than spend hours on the road to networking events.

They will also use their social media circles to validate information and may even discuss solutions with other businesses facing similar challenges. While it's easy for people to learn the basics about nearly any subject online, they don't necessarily want to. The dark side of the information age is that there is too much information to absorb.

Instead, people seek out subject matter experts to act as a guide to a particular field of interest. As you build your online presence educating others about the products and services in your market, you also position yourself as a niche-celebrity of sorts.

People follow you and are more likely to respond to your recommendations because of your positioning and when you visit your prospects and clients you can use your "celebrity niche status" that you've built up online to give you the edge over the "Jo Average" sales person that you're up against – but more on that later!!

The Future Of Modern Day Selling

All of this leads to a radically new environment from days before the Internet.

Faced with a need, your prospects and clients first port of call will be a search on the Internet to get a basic lay of the land for their problem and to find possible solutions and information.

Do you show up anywhere when someone searches for your products and services?

I'm not just talking about Search Engine Optimisation for your main company site here. Instead, I'm talking about blog posts, forums, videos – are you leaving a trail?

Where will prospects go to find out more information about their "pain"? Are there groups on Facebook or LinkedIn? If so, are you there too?

eselling®

The Future Of Modern Day Selling

They will also use Facebook and other busy social media sites to speak with other friends and acquaintances, or they will find discussion groups where your customers are already talking about your products, or the products of your competition.

Instead of your clients and prospects saving their questions for your meeting and PowerPoint presentation, they will be ready to talk about what is really going on behind the scenes!

This will be consultative selling to an evolutionary degree.

No longer will your clients and prospects wait for you to tell them about how your product will help them. Your meetings will be about how you, and your business, will deliver on those solutions and add value.

SEAN MCPHEAT

And before they meet with you they will do a search to check up on you as well.

As illustrated in the buyer research diagram below, your buyer is likely to be well-informed by the time you're even aware of them.

They will typically identify their own needs in terms of what they want and why they want it. This doesn't mean that they are correct in their identification of what they want and why, but it does mean they are probably further along in the thought process than people you may have worked with before the days of the Internet. It also means they have a bias to what they already believe to be true.

This is why eselling® is so important.

By positioning yourself as a thought leader, you can help provide the education your buyers are seeking online to "independently" make these determinations.

Next, the buyer begins to do research online. Just as you can use Google to seek out discussion forums and find resources to tell you what is being discussed about your marketing, so too can your buyer. They will seek out knowledge online through a variety of sources, but most of them are likely to be found in the first page of search results from Google for a particular keyword.

Through this research, the buyer will find new "friends" through social media and even online experts as sources of data. Your goal is to be one of these experts, providing the information your buyer is discovering online.

As the process unfolds, the buyer begins to actively engage his or her network through the discussion forums, LinkedIn Answers, Twitter, Facebook and any other online hangout he or she happens to use. This activity takes on the form of questions and conversations about the solution being sought after.

I have a friend who was working on a web-based video conferencing system.

On my suggestion, he went to http://search.twitter.com and searched for "video conferencing".

At the top of the results, was a message from a person literally stating that he was looking for a web-based video conferencing system and wanted suggestions.

Talk about a golden opportunity!

The process escalates as the buyer trims down the list of options and resources.

Web pages are often printed out and stuffed into a folder along with written notes – usually yellow post-its – and contact information for prospective vendors are collected too.

It's the digital dossier and it's the hallmark of the 21st century!

Keep in mind that the buyer is busy and is probably doing this research in the midst of many other job duties.

The entire process illustrated may take place over a few weeks, or days, but don't be surprised to find out that the entire process happened during a lunch break.

The next step in the process involves contacting vendors and suppliers and making enquiries.

Where do you think the contact information for potential vendors came from?

The buyers aren't calling information or looking up numbers in the phone book anymore. They're looking at the web page Google led them too.

If your contact information isn't obvious and easy to find, you're likely to be passed over.

Are you beginning to appreciate how damaging it can be for potential buyers not to be able to find you online and see exactly how to contact you without digging for your phone number?

The questions asked are also influenced by what was uncovered during the research phase.

Imagine if you had a blog post with the "top ten questions people should ask before buying X". Your new lead may be asking those questions, word for word, when calling you for more information.

There's an additional benefit to building a strong online presence through the eselling® model.

When reporters and media producers need an expert for an interview, where do they go?

They head straight to Google and look to see who is putting out the best content on a subject. They monitor Twitter to see who is talking about key subjects.

Who are the clear thought leaders?

Best doesn't mean the highly produced and over-polished celebrity wannabe.

It's about who has the "IT" factor that makes them a good fit for an interview in print, in front of the camera or the microphone.

That means that the more you position yourself with such media, the more you'll be seen as a leader in your field. What results is a snowball effect that further propels your authority as an expert in your field.

I bet you're thinking "But I sell franking machines into businesses, how is this applicable to me?"

Let's just take a step back and think about this.

Most of the machines on the marketplace are roughly the same so what is going to make the difference?

Superior service?

Nope – the "other guy" said that too.

A 3-year guarantee?

Nope – the "other guy" said that too.

20 years in the industry?

Nope – the "other guy" said that too.

12-hour call-outs?

Nope – the "other guy" said that too.

I could go on and on!

With this type of product, there's not much flux on the price and all of the "bells and whistles" are the same no matter who you engage with!

The difference is going to be the emotional attachment with a certain "brand", the positioning of the sales person and the quality of their sales skills.

Assume that you went online to research a franking machine and you came across a forum where someone was giving great advice on all types of products. They ran a Q&A session for small businesses about how to reduce their postage costs, the features and benefits of some of the main models out there and the like.

You might have sent that person an email as they seemed to know what they were talking about and you also did a search on that person's name and it led you to his own personal blog as part of the company. On this site you saw a TV clipping of him on the local news talking about reducing postage costs in the recession for small businesses, how you can use a franking machine for branding and how you can have complete control of your postal requirements.

All of a sudden this person is the "GO TO" person!

You engage him (let's call him Salesperson X) to come and see you along with another Salesperson from competitor Y.

Before Salesperson X turns up to meet with you, he sends you a short online video clip via an email about the product that you're interested in and it's actually him talking about it and demonstrating the product.

He also sends you a "one pager" about himself and how he has helped hundreds of small businesses to optimise what they are doing in terms of saving time and costs.

Salesperson Y does none of the above and just turns up.

So, before either of them has even spoken to you in person, let me ask you a quick question:

Who's in the lead at this stage?

Yes, Salesperson X is in front by a mile.

This is the beauty of eselling®. And this is EXACTLY what eselling® is about.

It's about making the Internet work for you.

Why People Don't Buy

To provide a useful resource for sales and marketing professionals, it's important to not only describe how to build a presence and sell, but also to explain why people may not buy at all.

While it may seem that the reasons not to buy are as varied as snowflakes, they all come down to one of three categories.

- They don't want it

- They can't afford it

- They don't believe you

All of these elements are often not what they seem on the surface and can be addressed through the benefits of eselling®.

Let's break each down further and get back to basics for a moment!

They Don't Want It

It amazes me how many people think that they have a product or service that every single person on the face of the earth desperately wants. If this was true, bottled water would have 100% market share. Everyone wants water. Everyone needs water. Not everyone buys it. While that may seem like a simple example, it holds true over and over again.

Of course, some examples seem more obvious than others. No matter how much chrome plating you add and how fast you make it go, it's very unlikely you will find anyone to buy your automatic eye-gouging machine.

It's just not going to happen!

There's no market for your product.

As basic as this concept may seem, far too many businesses go under because they fail to answer the question "Does anyone want this product?"

A great thing about eselling® is that you can use your ability to engage others online to have a conversation about issues like this. When you hold a conversation, people don't like to feel they're being sold to but they love to be heard. Conducted correctly, your conversation about a product, either existing or future can build a hungry, buying audience.

Apple has been doing this for years with amazing success.

Long before the advent of the iPhone and iPad, Apple spoke about the vision of the computer as a general appliance. They spoke of a computer that was used without the need for a manual and could be operated in a natural way, instead of requiring users to conform with its restrictive interface.

The sharing of this vision put the already fanatic customer base into a similar visionary state. Developers wrote software that approached this ideal as closely as the current technology would allow. They also provided feedback through the developer channels and pushed Apple to deliver on its vision.

When the iPhone was released, lines of people wanting to be the first to experience this new product queued up around the block.

In B2B sales environments, the same can be accomplished. As a solutions partner, you and your customers can craft new solutions and move your own offerings into larger markets, or create premium offers you may have never considered on your own.

Having a directed, and trusted, ear of your customer can lead to massive growth in directions you may never have expected.

They Can't Afford It

This is one of the most common excuses and yet it masquerades the real truth.

What they're really saying is that their perceived value does not match up with a price that you are asking. Because perceived value is lower than the asking price, the response you get is "I can't afford it."

Given the right motivation and the right value proposition, people can justify just about anything. In a depressed economy one might think that people would only buy the things they absolutely need. Yet flat screen TVs, smart phones, video games and products of all shapes and sizes continue to fly off the shelves. This is because the perceived value of these items is equal to or greater than the price.

It really is that simple.

As you develop content as part of your eselling® strategy, it is important to convey the value of what you have to offer. Value is not simply a numbers game. Even when you are selling to another business, emotional factors come into play in every purchase decision. You may think that your customers are different, but the reality is that the human brain is simply not wired to make decisions based on only rational thinking. Logic and emotion are processed by separate portions of the brain and the logic centre of the brain has less control over actions then the emotional centre.

Value feeds into a number of emotional triggers so don't ignore issues like prestige, importance and satisfaction just because you're dealing with business clients.

Value vs cost shows up in other ways too. Today, an email address is a form of currency. If visitors to your blog, or website, see your request to join your mailing list, but don't see enough value to do so, they're not going to "spend" their email address.

(By the way, in your email signatures too, you should be having links through to any free reports that you offer, your blog etc.)

eselling®

Time is also a form of currency and will impact how long a person watches a video, attends a seminar, or reads any of your articles or blog posts. Your clients and prospects see the adoption of your solution as work no matter how self-installing, auto-piloting and self-configuring it may be.

They are currently busy without your solution and from that viewpoint what you are selling is an addition to that busyness.

The more quickly you can establish value, the better. The more consistently you demonstrate value, the more people will trust the value of your content more implicitly. However, the value you convey needs to be in terms that are of value to your clients and prospects. The values devised by the marketing department, and printed on the data sheets, may not be the values most sought after by your customers.

This is why you need to engage them in dialogue and create an environment of trust so they'll tell you what's really going on.

They Don't Believe You

This is a big issue and can really waste a lot of your selling time because it's very rare that a person will come out and say this to your face.

Instead, a lack of belief leads to phone calls being unanswered, emails being ignored and appointments mysteriously postponed indefinitely.

Polls have shown that people are sceptical about everything they find online.

This is ironic, of course, because these same people use the Internet as their main source of information and research!

SEAN MCPHEAT

Yes, people are looking for product reviews and recommendations through the search engines and social media sites, but that doesn't mean they accept what they read or hear without question.

Instead, the behaviour seems to be one of seeking out a big picture.

This is why it's so important to create a large Internet footprint for yourself. One article or press release isn't enough. People are seeking a larger narrative from multiple sources.

Even if those sources are from you, the repetition is what gets the results.

By creating content that positions you, your products, your company and your market (if necessary) in the context you see it in, you are providing a counter to possible negative opinions being shared by other people.

These negatives can come up in the same Google search that shows your information. If there's a balance, there's a good chance that a person will look at more than one source of information and make an "independent and informed decision".

If there's no negative information, that doesn't mean there won't be. If you start to make an impact online, sooner or later someone else is going to say something negative about you, your products, your company or your market in general. By having your own content at the ready, you help to squelch those negatives and influence others with your view.

Transparency is the key to believable content.

The public is cynical when it comes to the presentation of information. The more authentic you are, the more credible you appear. The more slick and polished you look, the more they'll look for a reason not to believe you. Be real about what your products do and don't do. Be authentic about who you are and what values drive you. Show your values through your actions and build customers on a strong foundation of trust equity.

eselling® Uncovered

eselling® is not a new series of tactics for dealing with prospects' objections.

As a sales professional, you should already understand the basic principles of how to help other people solve their problems with what you have to offer.

Instead, eselling® is an approach for developing an online presence that you can use in all of your selling efforts (both online and offline), and it will help you to build up the trust necessary to break through the defences and barriers erected by people against your attempts to connect with them.

As the saying goes, when all things are equal people like to buy from those that they know, like and trust. All things being unequal, people still like to buy from those they know like and trust! When you meet someone new and hand them a business card, chances are very high that they will type your name into Google before ever returning a phone call or email. If you don't have a strong online presence, you're a ghost.

I believe that most people are very sceptical about sales people. Maybe it's got something to do with the fact that you know that if they don't sell then soon enough they will most likely be out of the job. And you wonder where their motivation comes from?

Is their motivation coming from the direction of actually helping you even if their product/service is not the right one, in which case they should tell you that, or does their motivation come from the fact that they "want to close you" no matter what?

eselling®

Yes, people don't like sales people much. But they do love experts and that's where eselling® can make a real difference.

eselling® shows you how to build an online presence and personal brand as a subject matter expert. It helps you to create and build a personal brand with which people can identify, relate to, or at least connect with.

eselling® shows you how to increase your Internet footprint online. Each piece of content is branded with you and points your readers and viewers back to more detailed information on you, your products, your company and your offers.

In building this online empire, you're better able to create new leads and close more sales as you meet your target buyers online.

This model recognises the way that people are using the Internet to research products, technologies, services, prices and even you personally before making a purchase decision.

eselling® is also about networking and prospecting online.

Armed with all of the blog posts, the videos, the whitepapers, the articles and so forth you can start to use sites like LinkedIn and Facebook to hunt out the people who you want to do business with.

You can do this directly or you can have a multi-contact strategy to engage that C-Suite Director that you want to get in front of. You'll do this by "giving" first and in return you will be establishing yourself as the expert.

After all, you'll have a lot of content to share!

Remember, networking is like dating. You have to take it in stages.

SEAN MCPHEAT

You'll never get anywhere if you ask for the "home run" on the first date!

Instead you need to build up your credibility and your trustworthiness over time.

We've got a whole chapter on how to prospect and network using social media so watch out for that one.

You can also use your Internet presence to position yourself offline too and you can use the Internet's "tools" to set you apart from the pack.

eselling® Examples

To give you a feel for the eselling® approach, here are some hypothetical examples of how different sales professionals could use various online options to build a strong presence and establish authority and trust with potential prospects and customers.

eselling® Example For A Commercial Estate Agent

Imagine you're an agent for commercial property.

You could build your presence by creating content to position yourself as an authority for your local area.

Starting with a blog, you could write articles, or report on, local developments in the pipeline, major purchases made in the previous month, development projects and even incentive programmes that could be of benefit to potential buyers.

Using the social media review site, yelp.com (for the US) or a site like welovelocal.com or touchlocal.com (for the UK), you could write reviews of local businesses and commercial properties in your area.

Even though you may not be selling these establishments, you are clearly establishing yourself as a person who knows, and is a part of, the local community.

Simple videos shot with a Flip Video camera can be uploaded to your free YouTube account or your blog.

Take a property and do a walk through. Don't shoot a commercial. Instead, create a tour that shows that you understand what clients really look for in a property.

Be honest and authentic.

If there's a part that is ugly to you, say so instead of creating euphemisms that signal a lack of candour to your audience. Just because you think something is ugly doesn't mean that others will feel the same or that they'll reject the property because of it.

Show the telephone cabling/server room, the wiring for the network, the toilets and even the shower if there is one!

What odd artifacts have been left behind by the previous occupants?

The property you're showing may be sold by the time a viewer stumbles upon the video so find ways to create extra value by being instructive or engaging through your video.

Also, photo sharing sites like Flickr.com give you the ability to share thousands of photos which you may never dream of posting for a more formal property listing.

Each photo is like virtual property pointing back to you as the source. Shoot pictures of the access roads, the roof, the back stairs and every part of the property that a customer is going to discover sooner or later. These are all a part of the environment.

SEAN MCPHEAT

As you collect video and picture content, create new content that provides new information and awakens interest based on the examples you've collected.

For example, you could show the communications room of all of the properties you've visited.

What should a client be looking for when it comes to such essentials in a property?

While this may not seem like an important subject on the surface, it's an essential to employees and anyone else who visits a property. What advice can you share that uses what you have to offer as a backdrop for the experience and wisdom you have to share?

So all of sudden you are THE ONLY commercial estate agent in the local area who runs a video blog with live showcases. You send your prospects a video of each property before they even show up, you've written 76 articles on how to select the right commercial property for your business and when you type in "Commercial Property Coventry", for example, in the search engines, you're all over the rankings commenting on various forums and blogs and if anyone types in "Commercial Property Expert" you're very own site is well up there in the rankings.

Yes, you've risen above the title of Commercial Estate Agent that all of your competitors hold and you are now in the "expert" and "trusted advisor" category.

And as they say in Ghostbusters: "Who ya gonna call?"

eselling® Example For Photocopier Sales

I've mentioned this example in the past.

A demonstrable product like a photocopier can lend itself to a broad portfolio of content possibilities.

Starting with a blog as a home page is again the best practice. From here you can talk about current issues, provide helpful advice and even offer new solutions related to communications through print.

The blog could be made up of articles, videos, demos and audios.

I remember when my own business introduced "proper" photocopier/printer machines instead of everyone in the office having their own printer and I was stunned to find out exactly what these machines could do!

If I'd have been educated over time there is no doubt in my mind that we'd have changed a lot sooner.

I remember saying to one of my team "Why didn't we get one of these years ago?" only to receive the reply "We never knew that these machines could do all of this!"

These machines can copy, print, scan, fax, print on both sides, make booklets – the list goes on!

And this creates the opportunity to educate your audience with new solutions that may go well beyond the needs of just a printer and a copier. So share your ideas and case studies through your blog.

Include pictures and videos whenever possible.

Again, the point of developing a strong online presence to support your eselling® efforts is to deliver value to your clients and prospects, increase your authority and credibility and close more sales.

Create content on topics which support the use of, and benefits from, your product.

Here are some examples of content you could create that support your expertise in the field of print media.

- 6 personal printers vs 1 all-purpose printer for the office: what's the pay off?

- How much time does an all-purpose printer save your company in 1 year?

- Advantages of recycled vs new fibre content

- How to make the best use of colour and double-sided print

- Double-sided printing vs single-sheet printing: the results of the survey are out!

- What's inside a copier (great for pictures and video)

Keep in mind that even in a B2B setting, a little personality can go a long way.

For some reason people seem fascinated with copying their face (or even their bottom!) so why not put together a tongue-in-cheek article on how to copy one's face with the best quality?

Done well, you may find your readers sharing your article through email, Twitter and Facebook and where might such viral exposure lead?

Video it and you could have a "Most Popular" video on YouTube within days receiving thousands of views.

Any product or service that results in time savings or cost savings are of interest to business owners. So why not approach popular business-related blogs and ask them if you can write an article or shoot a video for their audience on how much time and money an all-purpose copier could save them.

You could position it in light of the current economic climate: "How to reduce your printing costs by 20% in the recession".

This would not be an out-and-out plug for your own product although you'd have links to your blog underneath it. But you need to "hang out" where your prospects and clients hang out and if you sell to businesses then you absolutely must get involved in business-related blogs and forums.

Remember, the more you can educate your prospects and clients, the more trust you will build up with them. With the example above you could even provide the viewers with a free CD or free report at the end of the video. This creates free leads for you too!

Take it a step further and you could even approach your local news provider about doing an interview on the evening news business section of the programme about how small business owners are optimising their costs and that printing is one of those areas etc.

What benefit will this have for your selling?

Well, here goes:

- Free exposure to potentially thousands of viewers

- Take a screen shot of you on TV and post it on the header of your blog – instant street cred. "You've been on TV so you must be good"

- Use your photos on any articles that you post on others' blogs and forums

- Use it on your email signatures and in any information that you send your prospects before meeting with them

That's what eselling® is all about!

eselling® Example For Prospecting Online

Let's assume that you've developed lots of content.

You've got a blog and contribute regularly to it. You produce 1 video per month and you upload that to your blog and also to YouTube. So you've got lots of personal branding and positioning material in place.

You're an IT Consultant and you sell large-scale IT infrastructure solutions.

You've got 100 connections on LinkedIn and you want to target IT Directors.

Using the techniques that I will show you in "Get Social", you search for IT Directors in LinkedIn and you narrow down the results to 150 "qualified" IT Directors that you want to target.

You then research the LinkedIn groups that they are a part of and start to contribute to the discussions and start to position yourself as the expert, answering any questions they have posted, responding to threads they have left and so on.

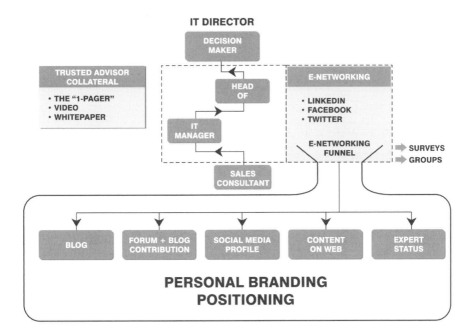

For those Directors that are not part of any groups but you have shared connections with you put a plan in place to get introduced to them via your shared connections.

Over time, you become "friends" online with the Director and become connected. You add them to your prospecting list and when it comes to the re-tender process for their infrastructure requirements they invite you in.

Now to get in front of this person via cold calling would have been virtually impossible with the quality of gatekeepers around nowadays but because you knew the correct way to network online and have proved your value over time, this was achieved and now you have the chance to tender on a £2 million contract.

Well worth the effort!

Who Is eselling® For?

eselling® is certainly not limited to the three examples in the previous section.

It can be used by any sales and marketing professional and especially for business-to-business (B2B) sales people who want a different and modern approach to generating leads and selling.

As a sales professional you already have a level of expertise in the products and services that you represent. Through eselling® you share that expertise online providing a benefit to those who need a solution to the types of problems that you solve.

Even in business-to-business transactions where there is a lot of buying criteria already imposed by the company, there's still a human element. Selling always involves people. No matter what kind of product or service that you're selling, a person does the research to solve the needs of the company. At some point it's a person making a request for the purchase. You have meetings with people to discuss the deal. A person shakes your hand and looks you in the eye. A person signs the PO and makes arrangements for payments.

But before any of this happens though, there's a person who visits the Internet to ask questions and conduct research on the solution the business needs.

Where are they finding the information they're looking for?

Today, it's not from your corporate website that probably still looks like a sales brochure with boring facts and figures.

Instead, they're going to YouTube, they're reading from forums and doing searches on Twitter and LinkedIn to see what other people and other customers – in some cases – are saying about how to solve their problems. They're mentioning products by name. They're mentioning people by name. They may be talking about you and your products right now. In short, they are researching possible solutions to solve their problems and they are educating themselves on the remedies at the same time.

eselling® is about stepping into this on-going process to join the conversation and to help provide the education your customers are seeking, and doing this where they are looking for it.

Effective esellers have built up a trusted authority position online and can be quickly vetted through the search engines prior to a sales meeting.

The eselling® Model

There are 10 activities that make up the eselling® approach.

Each one in its own right will dramatically improve your effectiveness as a sales professional. Combine the activities and you'll soon create your own online powerhouse!

Keep in mind that while much of this takes place online, eselling® is not dependent on you or your own business owning a website or having specific software – although it is a huge advantage if you do.

Some businesses can benefit greatly from picture sharing through sites like Google's Picasa, Yahoo's Flickr and Facebook's photo sharing features.

Using an inexpensive digital camera, it's easy to take pictures of new products, show details of individual parts, show people using the products, production facilities, and staff.

If you feel that your business truly has nothing to share through pictures, then don't force its use into your eselling® approach.

Focus on the other pieces and master them. As you do, look at what other people are doing with services and you may find that your own ideas will come along for how to use such services.

Let's recap what the eselling® approach will achieve for you:

- eselling® puts you back on the map – the one people are using today to find you

- eselling® positions you online as an authority in your field

- eselling® builds trust between you and your clients and prospects

- eselling® expands your reach and funnels leads towards you

- eselling® enables you to network and prospect online in the right way

eselling®

So let's move on and cover the **10 activities of eselling**® and they are:

- Understanding Your Space

- Establishing Your Personal Brand

- Create An Internet Footprint

- Get Social

- Enter The Conversation

- Positioning The Maven

- Building A Tribe

- Listening For Leads

- Embedding Your Brand

- Rinse, Wash, Repeat

Now you know what they are, let's cover each one in detail…

Understanding Your Space

The Internet is a gold mine of information for those with the patience and know-how to do a little digging! This information can help you to snoop up on the competition, it can help you to understand your prospects and clients better, it can help you to understand their needs and wants and lots more besides!

Before visiting a client or a prospect, do a search on Google. Chances are they did the same thing to you before confirming your meeting. What you find can give you enormous insight into what they're all about, what their concerns are, their buying triggers and even the types of things that might drive away the sale.

I'm not just talking about a search on their company here. Now that should be a given! But I'm talking about a search on the person that you are going to meet.

Are they on Facebook, LinkedIn or do they have a Twitter account?

If so you can find out a lot about them through their various profiles.

Before meeting with them you could find out things like they've only been in their current role for 3 months and previously they worked in an industry that you know very well. You might even find some common ground in terms of the people that they know and the people that you know.

On your LinkedIn profile and Facebook friends it might come up with people who are connected to you both. All of this information is very useful!

Using the Internet to listen is equally as important as building your own presence.

There are many tools available for listening and for collecting intelligence online.

Most of these tools are free as well.

Your ability to monitor client and industry activity with automated alerts and filters is your key to staying on top of the sea of information. You can then use that knowledge to help your customers and further earn their loyalty and trust.

In addition to keeping on top of client activity, use online searching and monitoring tools to keep up with competitor activity for your own business as well as for your clients. Don't be the fool who thinks you have no competition. If you think that no one does what you do, you may be suffering from a lack of imagination. Using these tools to keep an eye on your own market can prevent unpleasant surprises.

Listening In On the Internet and Social Media

There are lots of tools available for doing a quick check online. Master the basics before attempting to work with services that provide fancier options. In many cases, the advanced options won't seem so fancy if you have a feel for how to do your own searches. In other cases, you may appreciate a time-saving option that automates a series of well-defined searches.

When it comes to online searches and monitoring, some of the best services available are totally free.

Google

With over 60% of all searches going through Google, this is the best place to do your online research. Not only does Google provide most of the search data on the Internet, they also provide some of the best tools for working with them too.

In Google, you can search for web pages that match a particular phrase. You can also search for images, news items and blog posts.

Start out by visiting Google.com or Google.co.uk and search for your own name.

Take note of the search results and see where your name is showing up.

Don't just stick to page one of the results. Most people won't go beyond the first page, but you should have an awareness of what could end up on the first page.

Next, click "News" at the top of the window and Google will show you any news items that contain your name, or anyone with your name.

Repeat this basic procedure for any product name, company name or discussion topic that is useful for your business or the business of your clients.

As you get a feel for the kinds of results that come from different searches, you can delegate a more regular search to an associate or seek an automated service to do the searches for you.

Google.com/alerts

This free alert service from Google allows you to create searches which run continuously.

Each time there is something new found in the search, you can be notified through email. This provides you with an important and flexible business intelligence tool which can keep you up to date on any number of subjects.

Keep in mind that not everything that happens in the world appears on the web immediately, or in association with conveniently chosen keywords.

Setting up alerts can give you an enormous advantage over those who don't, but it is possible that events will happen which don't show up in a search.

I've got them set up for:

- My name

- My competitors' names

SEAN MCPHEAT

- My clients' names so I know any news that's going on with them

- Industry news

- Newly announced speaking gigs that I may want to approach

- Key phrases like "looking for sales training" "sales training" and many others!

If I were you I'd set up a Google alert for your name, your company name, the products/services you sell and any phrases that anyone might chat about in a forum or a blog about what you sell.

For example, you could set up an alert for "looking for an all-in-one printer"

Anytime that phrase is indexed on the web, you will be notified and you can then go to that page and join in the conversation or add them to your prospect funnel.

You could put in several different phrases similar to that:

"I'm looking for an all-in-one printer"

"I want an all-in-one printer"

"My all-in-one printer is broken"

"Anyone know any decent all-in-one printers?"

You get the picture!

So, I urge you to start using Google Alerts! Use it for online intelligence and for listening out for potential opportunities.

Google alerts **Manage your alerts**

Search terms	Type	How often	Email length	Deliver to
	Everything	as-it-happens	up to 20 results	Feed / View in Google Reader
"personal brand"	Everything	as-it-happens	up to 20 results	Feed / View in Google Reader
Home Business	Everything	as-it-happens	up to 20 results	Feed / View in Google Reader
Social Media	Everything	as-it-happens	up to 20 results	Feed / View in Google Reader

Search.twitter.com

Though you may not think of Twitter as a search engine, the number of searches made through Twitter has exceeded the number of searches through Yahoo and Bing combined.

The information you will find through Twitter does not directly include web pages, blogs and other forms of content but it may include discussions about such content and pointers to such things.

The content you find through Twitter will have a decidedly different feel from what you'll gain through the Google alert searches.

What you're seeing through Twitter is the result of discussions happening in real time.

Sometimes those conversations may be a bit one-sided, but you are seeing into the heart of the population. You may be amazed what you find.

SEAN MCPHEAT

More Online Intelligence Tools

Here's a list of other tools that will help you study and monitor trends and any mentions of key phrases online. There's no need to use them all. Some tools simply click better with some people compared to others.

Addictomatic (http://www.addictomatic.com/) This site provides a meta search and allows you to see what people are saying about a keyword through Twitter, YouTube, FriendFeed, Bing, Google, Digg, Delicious, Yahoo and more. The results are chosen as "top hits" based on an unknown heuristic. However, it can be a useful summary panel for popular topics.

Bloglines (http://www.bloglines.com/) Bloglines allows you to combine news and blogs into a single view through a web page or some smart phones. By using a service like this, you can get a panel view of important news and make scanning and keeping up to date a less time-consuming process.

Buzoo (http://buzzoo.net/ui/) Buzoo shows you the hottest stories at any given time based on various measures of current trends. While these stories may not directly relate to your own business, it can give you a quick insight into what the world is chattering about for your own general knowledge or as inspiration for blog posts and other content you'll be creating.

Blogpulse (http://blogpulse.com/) This is another trend-monitoring service that focuses on blog content. It includes tools which will graph trends and even compare different keywords to give you a feel for where the real conversations are taking place.

Board Tracker (http://www.boardtracker.com/) This site is worth checking out if you're looking to position yourself as an online authority. Unlike the many other tools that monitor the high profile social media sites like Facebook and Twitter, this service monitors the discussion groups and forums for mentions of your specified keywords.

Friendfeed Search (http://friendfeed.com/search/advanced) Friendfeed is known as a feed aggregator. People use it to combine the activities from other social media sites into a single stream of "news." This information includes videos, restraint reviews and a wide array of other types of content.

Hoot Suite (http://www.hootsuite.com) With this tool, you can send status updates to Twitter, LinkedIn, and Facebook from a single interface. You can also create columns to show you the feeds from these sites, with filters to narrow the results. It's a single window view of the most active sites you're likely to use and monitor.

Compete (http://www.compete.com) This is a web analytics service that allows you to monitor websites for levels of traffic, and search engine marketing competition.

Keyword Research

To figure out what people are talking about and looking for online, you will need to master the concept of keyword research.

Although keyword research is synonymous with internet marketing, as a sales professional you can really use this to your advantage.

This is something you can eventually delegate to others but it is something you must also understand for yourself as this represents the fundamental manner in which data and information is being stored and retrieved through the Internet.

As you find new keywords, you will use them in your blogs, videos, and even the summary field of your LinkedIn profile. This causes your pages to come up when people look for those keywords. Once they're on your page – or virtual property – you can invite them to action by asking them to call, sign up, click a button or whatever else makes sense within your strategic approach.

Two factors apply when it comes to getting more visitors.

The quality of your keyword research and the amount of content you're creating.

Every new piece of content is like virtual property. Any one piece may only get found a few times a day for tightly focused keywords, but if you have hundreds of such properties then that adds up to a bonanza of free traffic to your blog, videos and website.

Even if you're only focused on positioning yourself online, people vetting you are going to see your content everywhere.

That helps establish trust and authority online.

What Does Keyword Research Mean?

At its heart, the nature of keyword research is to find a match between your target customers and your own business using what they're searching for and talking about online.

In some cases, you may find that the keyword phrases you think are important are not being searched for at all and if no one is looking for you based on a particular keyword, what good is it to invest time and effort creating optimised content around it?

For example, if you were to compare the numbers of searches for "Toastmasters" to the number of searches for "public speaking", there's almost no comparison.

Public speaking wins without the need for a second look.

What does this mean for an organisation dedicated to helping people improve their public speaking skills like Toastmasters International?

Obviously they should be developing online content focused on the keyword "public speaking" and use it as a bridge to help people discover Toastmasters.

This may seem obvious but many businesses completely mess up here by focusing their efforts on optimising their websites and other content around words and phrases which are important to their company but of no interest to anyone else.

The principle of this is simple:

"If you want people to find you, go to where they are and speak using their words!"

How To Research Your Keywords

Keyword research involves finding the phrases that match what people are looking for online and what you have to offer.

If your product name or brand isn't being searched for much, use more popular – and related – keyword phrases to build a bridge between what people are looking for and what you have.

To be effective, keyword research requires an open mind and creativity and a love of the hunt. You'll be looking for phrases that are being searched for online with some regularity. This number is highly variable and depends highly on your market.

You also want phrases that don't have a lot of other web pages competing for the top spots in the search results if possible.

Long Tail vs Short Tail Keywords

A keyword can be a single word or an entire sentence.

The types of keywords on which you focus can make a big difference in your results and in the responses you get from people visiting your web pages.

When doing keyword research, you will begin with a single word, or a very short phrase that conveys what your target customers would be looking for online.

For example, the word "golf" could be your starting point for golf equipment.

This is known as a short tail keyword. If you do a search for *golf* through Google, you will find there are millions upon millions of pages which contain this word.

How would you ever get your content found on the first page of these results?

The answer is simple: you don't even bother.

There are a few reasons for this.

For one, the competition for such a short phrase is enormously high. It would require substantial time and resources to gain the No.1 position for a keyword like this.

Second, there's no real value in doing so. People searching for only

golf are not motivated buyers. They're simply browsers with no intention to join a mailing list or to make a purchase.

Third, there's a negative cost associated with these short tail keywords. Because your traffic from such a keyword is coming from sources that will convert very poorly, if at all, the resources for your web server are consumed by people that only cost you money.

The solution lies in the magic of the long tail keyword!

As you begin your keyword research with the tools mentioned in the next section, look for the longer phrases which contain your "short tail" or "root keyword" that convey literal questions or indications of motivation.

For example, while someone searching for "golf" may not be motivated to buy, someone searching for the following examples are far more likely to respond to a call to action.

SEAN MCPHEAT

- Best prices for Ping **golf** clubs

- Comparison of **golf** shoes

- How to improve my **golf** swing

- **Golf** training videos

- **Golf** vacation packages in Fiji

- Where to buy Nike **golf** shirts

Each one of these phrases may lend itself to a piece of content that you could create through a blog post, article, video or podcast content.

The long tail speaks directly of a person, which helps you create a connection between them and yourself.

What To Do With Keywords

As you find keyword phrases, build content around them.

Try to use a keyword in the headline or title of each blog post, video, or article you create for that item. Use the keyword two to three more times in the body of the text and in the description, as in the case of a video on YouTube. If the phrase doesn't read well, you're better off moving to another keyword.

Also, use the term in your tags too.

For the purposes of building your online presence, this is as far as you need to take things.

You can spend a lot more time worrying about exactly how many times to use a keyword, or other places to use it in the construction of a page. Your time is better spent moving to the next piece of content and building it.

These minor efforts take little time and put you ahead of 99% of the other content online for search engine optimisation.

Build your presence first and then take a course on advanced SEO if you feel the need. You can then go back and edit premium content for better search rankings.

It's very easy to go overboard with search engine optimisation. Yes, you do want to be found online. However, if you do this at the expense of creating valuable content that people will want to read, watch or listen to, the value returned on your efforts will be low.

eselling® is about positioning and relationship building online. As you gain followers and subscribers, these people will continue to see your new content regardless of your search engine rankings.

Think of keyword research as your way to most efficiently – and effectively – prime the pump with content that matches what people are looking for.

Keyword Research Tools

There are quite a few keyword research tools available but the ones mentioned below should provide you with everything you will need to find keywords with low to moderate competition and regular monthly search traffic.

As with everything, experiment first and get a feel for how things work. The insight you gain from keyword research is like looking at a giant ink blot test. You may see things that others will not, even looking at the same data.

In the context of this book, the purpose of these tools is to generate ideas for creating content and for sorting keywords that are of relative value to you.

For a more detailed instruction on doing keyword research for an Internet marketing campaign, seek out a class or other in-depth resource on the subject of Internet marketing.

Google Adwords Keyword Tool

Google Adwords keyword tool is one of the best because the data is coming directly from Google. As the search engine providing more than 60% of online search results, information from them is going to be very useful.

If you do a search for "Google Adwords Keyword Tool" it will take you to the page.

I haven't put the website address down for you because Google is in the process of changing it as I write this!

To use the tool, visit the website and enter a keyword into the search box.

In the example below, I've used "Coffee Mugs".

Now the beauty of this tool is that you can select the language and also the country where those searches are being made.

So if you are based in Brazil and sell coffee mugs then you can receive the number of searches being made just in Brazil if you like. Or if you are a worldwide company where location is not an issue you can include "All Countries" and "All Languages" with your search.

For this example, I've chosen English as the language and the location as the United States.

At the top is the phrase by itself – known as the root keyword – and some data to help us analyse it.

The total number of monthly searches covers all phrases that contain the words "coffee mugs".

In this case 6,600 isn't bad.

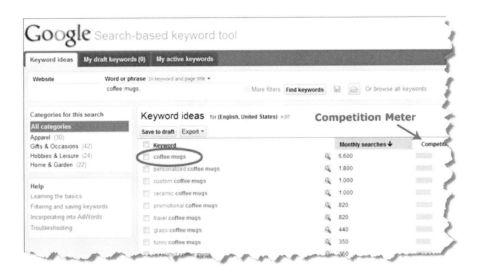

Keep in mind though, you may not need to worry about thousands of monthly searches as long as you're getting found by the right people.

The competition meter is nearly full for coffee mugs, which means that there are a lot of other web pages and pay-per-click advertisers fighting for dominance with this keyword.

However, notice a few spots down, ceramic coffee mugs has less competition.

This is what you want to be looking for: a keyword that is going to give you enough free traffic to get customers but in an environment where you don't have to fight for it.

The suggested bid column is the current highest-paying ad through Google pay-per-click advertising network. This value is very dynamic because PPC ads are run through an auction and advertisers have the ability to change their ads, bids schedule them for display, or pull them off at any moment.

However, this information can still give you insight into the popularity and viability of a keyword.

You may find a phrase that has very low competition, high monthly searches and is going for £0.10 a click through the ad network. Is this because the phrase is for an untapped niche or is it one that just doesn't perform?

Sometimes you'll need to use your gut to decide.

For further analysis, let's search for a couple of these keywords through Google and see how many other pages have been indexed by Google.

First, searching for *coffee mugs* shows there to be about 5,290,000 web pages that Google thinks might have something to do with coffee mugs.

coffee mugs

About 5,290,000 results (0.25 seconds)

Searching for *ceramic coffee mugs* reports 2,550,000 listings.

ceramic coffee mugs

About 2,550,000 results (0.34 seconds)

Another search for *ceramic coffee mugs*, with quotes around the phrase comes back with 62,200 results.

"ceramic coffee mugs"

About 62,200 results (0.33 seconds)

The difference between the two searches is caused by using quotes in the search.

Putting quotes around the phrase tells Google to show only pages that contain those words in the same phrase. Without the quotes, Google also considers pages that have all the words on the page, just not together.

So to build content that gets top rankings for the keyword *ceramic coffee mugs* your real competition is 62,200 other pages, not 2.5 million.

This is actually good news because some SEO experts have asserted that over 99% of the content on the Internet is put there with no effort to optimise it for search.

This means that of the 62,200 pages mentioning a ceramic coffee mug, only a handful may actually be doing so in an attempt to be found through search.

Repeat these steps and put your results in a spreadsheet.

You're building your game plan for content generation!

Google's Wonder Wheel

The Wonder Wheel view is a free tool that is really useful for building up your keyword databank. It will give you some ideas of related keywords that Google likes. So this is a useful tool for brainstorming and creativity.

After you enter a search phrase into Google, click "Wonder Wheel" in the options along the left hand side of the page. This will change you to the Wonder Wheel view which is signified by the spoked wheel in the centre of the page.

Each of the spokes points to another possible keyword that Google thinks may be related to the phrase you entered.

These aren't random suggestions. They are the result of Google's own analysis on the relationship between keywords and phrases it indexes on the web. Click on one of these phrases to go to another set of linked suggestions.

Notice how the suggestions at the spokes don't always contain the keyword you originally entered. This data is coming from Google's own algorithms. It's worth taking note of the phrases it believes to be related to your original search.

If this was it for the Wonder Wheel, it would be only of passing interest.

Click on one of the phrases at the end of a spoke to see where the real value comes in.

Each time you click a phrase, the Wonder Wheel will take you along a path of keywords. All of these are potential subjects for creating content. Not all of these keywords are money makers though.

eselling®

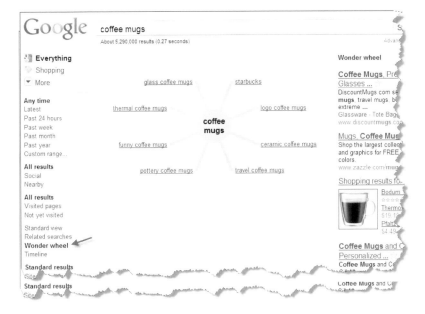

Put them through the Google Adwords keyword tool and check for completion to make sure you're working with a good bet.

So some additional keywords to add to your list will include:

- Wholesale Coffee Mugs

- Handmade Ceramic Mugs

- Ceramic Travel Coffee Mugs

- Personalised Coffee Mugs

- Ceramic Tea Cups

Wordtracker Free Keyword Tool

Even though Google has the most data on web searches, their tools don't give you everything you need for brainstorming content.

Wordtracker.com has a free and paid service that fills in the gaps left out by Google.

To use the free Wordtracker keyword tool, visit them at http://freekeywords.wordtracker.com.

Enter a keyword and click *hit me*.

Wordtracker gets search data from sources other than Google so the column showing the number of searches won't match what you might find from Google.

It doesn't matter because this information is used for brainstorming and prioritising.

Instead of simply entering your keyword, add the following words to the start of your search: who, what, where, when and why.

eselling®

how bbq 3,010 searches (top 100 only)	Want more *how bbq* keywords?
Keyword	**Searches (?)**
1 how to bbq ribs (search)	392
2 how to bbq pork ribs (search)	322
3 how long to bake bbq chicken (search)	275
4 how to bbq beef ribs (search)	211
5 how to bbq filet mignon (search)	199
6 how to cook bbq chicken (search)	165
7 how long to cook a hamburger on bbq (search)	132
8 how to bbq shrimp (search)	128
9 how to make bbq ribs (search)	123
10 how long to bbq chicken (search)	61
11 how to make bbq ribs in the slow cooker (search)	58

Start a new search for each of these words. The results are questions people are asking in association with your keyword. This is like a menu for content creation because these results are telling you what people are literally asking for online.

Additionally, you may also try entering your keyword with a question mark.

Also a space and then a question mark. This can show you some questions that somehow aren't showing up when using the other question words in your search phrases.

Wordtracker gets its data from search engines other than Google.

As a result, the numbers you see for total searches is a tiny fraction of what is really happening online. Use these numbers to get a feel for what people are looking for.

They're not to be used for calculations in a sales forecast.

SEAN MCPHEAT

So What Now?

After you have completed your keyword research you should be left with a long list of long tail keyword phrases.

We'll be using these in the "Creating An Internet Footprint" chapter, where you will be putting together lots of content to be found online when people search for your wares, and also for sending out to prospects and clients who are in your sales funnel for positioning and personal branding purposes.

Searching For Files Online With Google

It's time for you to be a secret agent spy!

Did you know that Google not only returns web pages in its search results but it also returns videos and documents too?

This can be very valuable to a savvy searcher like you're about to become!

Over the years I've been able to lay my hands on some very sensitive information that has been put up on the Internet.

I've been able to find word documents and PowerPoint proposals from my competitors! I've been able to find tender documents that hadn't even been released to the general public and I've been able to find manuscripts, whitepapers – you name it!

It's possible to find lots of different types of documents and files online talking about your products, customers and marketplace.

To conduct one of these searches simply enter the keyword into

Google followed by *filetype:* and the filename extension used to identify that file. Mac users may not be familiar with these filename extensions, and new Windows users may not see them due to the default settings in the file viewer.

Below are the common file extensions you can search for.

PowerPoint: <keyword> filetype:ppt

PowerPoint: <keyword> filetype:pptx

MS Word: <keyword> filetype:doc

MS Word: <keyword> filetype:docx

MS Excel: <keyword> filetype:xls

MS Excel: <keyword> filetype:xlsx

Adobe PDF: <keyword> filetype:pdf

Here's an example searching for PowerPoint files on "metal stress".

A file type search like this can be very handy for doing quick research on the types of issues experienced by a client or prospect.

Simply look at the types of information that's ended up in slides being used for presentations in their industry.

Why would you want to look for files online?

It's a great form of online intelligence.

You can find out what other people are already presenting when it comes to issues in your market.

metal stress filetype:ppt

About 4,860 results (0.28 seconds)

[PPT] powerpoint - Philip Hofmann ☆
File Format: Microsoft Powerpoint - View as HTML
stress/strain curve for a ductile metal. picture of how this is measured. 9. Macroscopic
picture: elastic deformation. the linear region ...
philiphofmann.net/book_material/lectures/lecture3_gen.ppt

[PPT] Module 7a - College of Engineering ☆
File Format: Microsoft Powerpoint - View as HTML
Determine the value of the strain-hardening exponent for a metal that will cause the averag
flow stress to be three-quarters of the final flow stress after ...
www.engr.usask.ca/...07/.../handout-7-metal%20forming_Mar1.ppt - Similar

[PPT] FUNDAMENTALS OF METAL FORMING ☆
File Format: Microsoft Powerpoint - View as HTML
Figure 18.6 Effect of temperature on flow stress for a typical metal. The constant C, as
indicated by the intersection of each plot with the vertical dashed ...

Searching For Blogs And Online Discussions

Blogs, online discussions and forums provide you with a real world view of what's on the mind of your target market.

Simply start with a Google search for your keyword and "blog". In the example, we'll look for blogs on printers. Some of the returned results may be for commercial printers and others may be for small office printers.

You'll need to expend a bit of effort to find the type you're looking for, but the quick search results from Google certainly makes this process easy compared to what it would take without them.

Google provides some additional filters to help narrow down the results for you.

eselling®

To specify that the results you want to see are only for blogs, click **More** in the area on the left.

The search results will change to reflect only what Google believes to be a blog.

It may exclude some useful blogs which is why you want to look at all of the results.

Use these options as an aid, but don't assume that just because you click Blog in the search list that Google is going to provide 100% infallible results.

Next, search for discussion forums.

Search for your keyword plus forum or discussion.

Using "printer forum" as an example, the results should be of discussion groups talking about printer issues.

Then click **More** and select **Discussions** from the list on the left.

Google will narrow the results to what it believes are specifically discussion forums.

How it makes such a determination is not specified but it will give you results that may not show up in the unfiltered list without a lot of extra work, so go over the filtered and unfiltered results and make a list of what looks useful to you from both.

Again your results will change a bit to reflect what Google thinks are only discussion forums.

You may find some results that didn't show up in the unfiltered list.

So what do you do with this information?

Well, you should read and study what people in your market are talking about.

SEAN MCPHEAT

Are there any current issues that they're talking about? Can you provide the forum with some useful information? Are the readers moaning about a certain make and model of printer? Are they using the forums purely for support purposes? Are they talking about your makes and models of printer? If so, is it good? Bad?

You may find some new sales opportunities simply by "listening in" to what is being written about. You're hunting for pain and dissatisfaction!

This shouldn't be a new concept to any sales professional. The online world simply gives you new ways in which to listen.

The threads also give you a fantastic heads up as to the types of content that would resonate well with the audience. So it gives you a lot more ideas for content generation, blogs and videos that you might want to put together.

Also, get involved yourself!

Pick the best blogs, forums and discussion boards that are most relevant to you and the ones with the most activity and then get stuck in.

But a word of advice...

Especially in the early days of your contributions go there to "give" rather than to "get". You'll need to build yourself up as a credible source, not just someone who is a chancer trying their luck.

If you look on any forum under each user then it normally says how many posts they've made to that forum. In the example below the user macnab has made only 1 post. This illustrates that they are a brand new user.

So get involved. Start creating your own discussion topics and also contribute answers to others. It's time to position yourself as an expert!

eselling®

Optimising Your Name For The Search Engines

Type your name into Google, Yahoo & Bing and where do you show up?

The results that you find are exactly the same that your prospects and clients will see if they were to perform a search on your name too.

Now if you've got a LinkedIn, Facebook or Twitter account and use your name as part of your username, for example http://www.linkedin.com/in/seanmcpheat then, because these sites are very powerful, chances are that one of these will most likely show up somewhere in the top 10 so you'd better make sure that your profiles on these sites do you justice, are full and that your photos do not include you face down in the gutter from last week's party!

Pay particular attention to your profiles on these sites because people will just love to snoop around and find out more about you. I'll cover what to include and how to manage these sites later in "Get Social".

SEAN MCPHEAT

In terms of other content produced by you, when you create the content online the search engines will look at all of the content and will use that to determine how to index it in their giant database.

If your name is not part of the content then your name will not be associated with it.

Some websites will help you circumvent this issue by providing a profile that gets indexed by the search engine and that links to all of the content you've created on that website.

Personal websites and blogs tend to be a little bit more fluid so you want to make sure that your full name is included somewhere in the content, the description, tags, meta keywords and maybe even in the title of the blog or article like:

"3 Ways To Reduce Your Printing Costs By Sean McPheat"

Another issue that can cause a challenge is if you have a very popular name.

Now my name is very unusual, but say your name was John Smith!

Just how many other John Smiths are out there?

Guess how many results Google returns for "John Smith"?

4.3 Million!

So what can you do if you have a popular name to make sure that you're found in the search engines?

Including your middle initial or adding a word or two describing your field of expertise in the proximity of your name may be necessary to help you get found.

eselling®

For example, if you are positioned as a document management specialist, make sure that is included in all of your profiles, the titles of your YouTube videos and anywhere else that you're creating content.

Manually create the association between your name and your field.

Pulling It All Together

With all of these online research tools at your disposal there can never be any excuse for you not to be well prepared and informed about your marketplace, your prospects and your clients.

You need to be well organised though to keep track of this information.

Here's what I would do if I were you:

1. **Set up a file for your existing clients.** Now this can be online or offline, whichever you prefer. Set up your Google alerts for each of them so you keep on top of everything that is happening with them. Set the alerts for daily updates first of all so you can gauge the volume of updates that you're going to receive. If it becomes too much make it a weekly update and review all of the updates in one go.

2. **Set up a file for your prospects.** Just like before, set them up for Google alerts and for some of the other approaches I've mentioned in this chapter.

3, **Set up a file for industry intelligence.** This is going to be the vault that houses information about what's going on in your industry, new technology, any awards coming up, any legislation that impacts your clients and prospects etc.

SEAN MCPHEAT

4. **Set up a spreadsheet for your keyword research.** The beauty of most of the tools I've covered is that you can download your keyword reports directly into a spreadsheet. Set up a spreadsheet with a new worksheet for each of the products and services that you sell and place the respective keywords in each. Remember, these keywords are going to form the basis of your online content so what you've got then is a list of the potential articles, blog posts or videos that you are going to produce.

5. **Set up a spreadsheet with relevant blogs, forums and discussion groups.** Mark down the ones that you are going to contribute regularly to and those that you will review a couple of times per month. Schedule when you will review the various blogs and forums into your diary.

6. **Set up a file for competitor analysis.** "Keep your friends close and your enemies even closer". Keep records and updates of what they are doing, what they are offering and any time they are in the news.

Check out these websites for free tools to help you save information you find on the web to an account you can access from your computer or most smart phones.

Evernote (http://www.evernote.com)

Instapaper (http://www.instapaper.com)

Both of these tools give you the ability to create "clippings" of information you find on the web for later sorting and retrieval.

Because information online can change in the blink of an eye, make sure that you save the information you find in some way.

Don't rely on Google providing you with exactly the same search results next week or next month. Information on the web is very dynamic and such things can, and do, change without any warning. Keeping your own files gives you an edge.

It's an information asset!

Remember, the information you can access online isn't significantly different than what you have been able to track for decades. It's just easier and much quicker to do!

No matter what filing system you choose to use, keep in mind that the online intelligence you collect is a valuable asset for you and for the sales process.

Just as you would send clippings of valuable information to a prospect or client through postal mail, you can do the same through email and social media.

Share some of the information you find. It positions you as an expert in your field and one that knows what's going on beyond the walls of your own office.

Establishing Your Personal Brand

The concept of a personal brand is becoming more and more important as people are meeting up and getting discovered online.

Your online presence leaves a digital footprint and shapes the perception others have of you when searching online for you, your products or your industry.

Whether you intend it or not, this activity helps establish your personal brand as people encounter you online. The more exposure they have of you, the more this relationship is strengthened and refined.

With a strong, consistent approach to personal branding, the right people will follow you while others may seek out a better match for themselves.

A weak, inconsistent approach to personal branding will result in nothing.

A strong personal brand can help you to stand out online and will help your efforts offline too. There are also many misconceptions when it comes to personal branding.

In this chapter I will explain what personal branding is and how it fits into the eselling® model.

What Is A Brand?

Before explaining what the concept of a personal brand is, it's helpful to begin with a discussion about product branding.

eselling®

Regardless of what colour the packaging is, the fonts and other style decisions, a brand is a relationship.

That relationship is between the product and a person.

While some may believe that the relationship can be with the community, the brand is still made up of individual relationships with each person in the community. This is a very important concept to grasp because while there may be similarities in that relationship among groups of people, no two are alike.

Imagine a well-known brand of soft drink and its simple red and white design for the artwork! While there have been minor changes over time the basic style of that artwork has remained the same for decades. The contents of the drink has also remained the same. From one generation to the next Coca-Cola is known for its consistency.

If this was the only part of the equation then you would expect the way that individual people perceive this product would be consistent as well. Yet, if you ask 100 people to provide you with words or stories describing their relationship with Coca-Cola, you'd get 100 different answers.

Individually you would hear stories about how some people absolutely love Coke and that they drink four or five cans a day.

You might even hear a story about the impact Coke was perceived to have had on a person's childhood and a relationship with their father. Someone might describe the logo as invoking the memory of good times since passed.

You would also find that some people prefer the taste of Pepsi to Coke or some people just don't like any type of cola.

Another person may be against the business practices of the company that makes the soft drink. You might hear people talk about dangerous chemicals, refined sugar and a host of other negatives whether those negatives are real or not.

A third group of people would represent the middle of the road. If Coke stopped selling tomorrow, they simply wouldn't mind too much. These people don't have any strong feelings for, or against, the product. Sometimes they buy and sometimes they don't.

Even though all of these people are looking at the same product, they do not share the same individual experience.

Each person's background and make-up is unique. Therefore the way that they experience a relationship with that brand is also unique.

Interestingly enough, the people who really don't like this product sometimes help to create as much word-of-mouth online buzz as the people who love the product.

Their attempts to expose the product and make others aware about its negative attributes end up attracting more of the people who love the product!

Although we know that everyone is different and that they have their likes and dislikes, many people will try to make everyone into a raging fan of the product!

Attempts to turn the detractors into supporters backfire at times.

The middle group is confused by brand inconsistency and stops buying the product altogether. The original "love it" crowd feels betrayed and they stop buying it too.

This is why one of the characteristics of a successful brand is **consistency.**

eselling®

As long as a product meets the needs of an actual market, it makes much more sense to remain consistent than to continually compromise in an attempt to be all things to all people.

What Is A Personal Brand?

First and foremost, a personal brand is not just about the clothes that you wear or how you've cut your hair. Sure, they contribute towards your persona but it's not your brand.

A personal brand is held in the relationship **between you and another person.**

As people are exposed to you, they develop an impression of you.

That impression influences how they hear you, the trust they have in you and what to expect from you.

Keep in mind that an effective personal brand does not have to be likeable.

Going out of your way to be disliked is a poor strategy for a sales career, but assuming that you must be liked by all people is an equally poor – and fruitless – approach.

As mentioned in the earlier discussion on product branding, it is more important that you seek consistency in your personal brand as well. Consistency leads to trust.

Yes, someone may find your personality grating, but if they know that they can count on you for whatever it is that you are known for, they're still likely to go with you. If they really don't like you, then it's probably better they work with a more compatible personality rather than making you both miserable for the rest of your professional lives!

SEAN MCPHEAT

Positioning Yourself As An Expert

People just love dealing with experts.

And many of the experts that you'll come across will have strong personal brands.

In my opinion many people are just begging to be led by someone who knows their stuff.

Now being an expert doesn't mean that you need a PhD in your subject!

In fact, some people who demonstrate skills that make them experts among experts have no formal education at all!

What you need to appreciate is that people are being bombarded with sales and advertising messages each and every day. They are overwhelmed with work, they are mostly overwhelmed with their home life too, and the uncertainty of the economy and all that goes with it means that they are looking for guidance and certainty in a non-certain world.

Now being an expert and having a wealth of knowledge and experience means nothing unless you can demonstrate and show how your "expert status" can help others.

It's really all about how you apply what you know to help others that provides a display of competence and engenders trust.

To establish yourself as a subject matter expert online, here are some guidelines to help you.

Stay Focused

It's ok to mention that you're heading to the gym on Twitter but it's going to do nothing to help establish you as an expert in your field.

Try to remain focused on content that actually shows your activity as a thought leader in your field.

Be Original

Activity on social media is a balance between being connected with other thought leaders in your field and having your own original thoughts to share.

If your Twitter status messages are an endless stream of "retweets" and links to content generated by others then you're not a thought leader, you're just another follower.

However, if you provide your own content and give recognition to others in your field with good ideas too, then you show that you have something to say and that your ego doesn't blind you to believe that no one else has anything to say.

Don't Sell, Sell, Sell!

If your content screams "buy my stuff" over and over again, you will be ignored.

It's really that simple. In the midst of providing value to your followers let them know when you have a new offer and include a link to a landing page or your blog etc.

Done sparingly, this practice is a good approach.

However, keep providing value through your social media presence to ensure that people continue to pay attention.

Do You Need Credentials To Be An Expert?

When it comes to credentials, use them if you have them.

Move on and shine anyway if you don't!

The reality is that the only people who consistently "check your credentials" are those who have them and want to protect their turf.

If you have the distinguished status as a speaker with Toastmasters International, broadcast it through your online presence. If you don't, then get up and speak anyway.

People love to follow thought leaders and the ideas that they share. That means you take what you know and create new views and visions with it. Ideas can be a catalyst for action. They can mobilise masses. They can enact great change.

As a thought leader, you're not just regurgitating the same information your prospects could pull up from Wikipedia. Instead, you provide the context and the vision to show others how what you do, and what you work with, is beneficial **to them.**

You show how it can change the lives of others and how it can make a difference to the buyer and their business.

The relationship a person has with a product brand is often shaped by more than the product itself and this is true of your personal brand as well. Some people will take note of how a company handles issues around touchy subjects like child labour, the environment and sustainable agriculture. As people Google you, they may also look for such personal details to round out their impression of you.

While you may choose to be quiet about more controversial topics like politics and religion, they're likely to come up sooner or later. How you want to reveal these things is up to you. Listing your affiliations in your Facebook profile may be enough or you may openly participate in discussion groups on your favourite topics.

As mentioned in the previous discussion on branding, don't assume that the public will view your personal brand in exactly the way that you intended.

The only thing you can do is manage your own behaviour and act according to your values.

Examples Of Strong Personal Brands

Donald Trump is viewed by many as a straight-talking, successful businessman.

His books sell well and his TV show "The Apprentice" still receives respectable ratings.

Some people love him and some people don't.

Does he try to win over those who don't?

In a word – no.

Donald Trump stands up for himself and does what he does.

Not all of his businesses have been successful. He's upfront and honest about this and he carries on making his businesses successful more often than not.

What is Richard Branson's brand?

He's maintained his approach to business through a series of companies under the Virgin label and some amazing stunts that nearly got him killed.

"... you run one company, you can run any company." Says Branson!

Many of his fans will describe him as a person who applies a youthful energy and vision to every venture. Based on the narrative from his books and public speaking appearances, that appears to be consistent with what he sets out to do.

Does everyone view him in that light?

No, and Richard Branson is savvy enough to realise that it's more important to follow his own values than it is to attempt to manipulate the opinions and views of others so they all conform.

As with Donald Trump, not all of Branson's efforts have been successful.

Did you buy a Virgin Cola?

Branson is willing to make mistakes in public which many people admire. It's a sign of authenticity and a strong character.

As you look at other public figures, or even a lesser-known person with a video blog on YouTube, there is no way to objectively declare the characteristics of their personal brand.

You can only observe your own experience of that person through the lens of your own perception.

Knowing this is a key to a strong personal brand as we explore the characteristics of a personal brand in the next section.

The Characteristics Of A Personal Brand

When evaluating the characteristics of a personal brand, the various ingredients that others see derive from a combination of three main categories: your values, your skills and your style.

Another way to word the latter two is to say it's what you do and how you do it.

These are typically a reflection of your values because it's your values that will most influence what you're most interested in and the passions that drive you to excel at one thing versus another.

No one of these characteristics is more important than another. They are all a part of the greater whole and support each other synergistically.

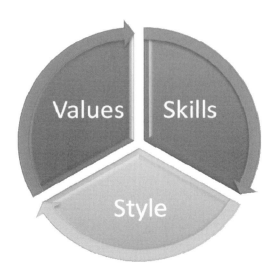

Your Values

Think about a soft drink for a moment.

Now values feed the ingredients for products as well as personal brands.

One soft drink company may use only natural ingredients in their products, avoiding all chemical preservatives and artificial sweeteners.

This is based on the values built into the company. Another company may feel that other "modern" ingredients are perfectly acceptable.

So what are your values?

Think about this carefully now because sometimes key values are easily overlooked.

For example, do you value truth and honesty at all costs?

How about compassion?

Honesty with a lack of compassion is a formula for cruelty. If you were to list your values in terms of priority what is at the top of the list and what's at the bottom?

Don't think of this self-evaluation in terms of right and wrong. The answers are yours and reflect how you interact with the world.

Values aren't something that you apply according to the season. They come from within and influence everything that you do.

Become more self-aware and observe yourself to determine what values are most important to you. If you find that your actions don't reflect the values that are important to you, or if you realise that there are some values that are more important to you than you first thought, then adjust accordingly.

Growth is a natural part of life and even the realisation of important values is a part of that process.

In this media-driven world, it's easy to find yourself programmed to act in a certain way because it's what you see others do and it's what the magazine articles tell you to do.

So look within yourself and work out what your values really are and become more conscious of how you apply them to your daily actions.

What do you do with these values?

You apply them... consistently!

Applied values are virtues. If you value candour as well as compassion, then practice speaking your mind in a conscientious and empathic manner.

To Do:

Work out what your values are.

Now there are hundreds of different values and it would be one huge complicated task if I gave 400 of them to you and then said "Ok, pick your top 10!"

So I've diluted the list down to give you a start.

Achievement	Integrity
Advancement	Involvement
Adventure	Loyalty
Affection	Order
Competitiveness	Personal Development
Cooperation	Pleasure
Creativity	Power
Economic Security	Recognition
Fame	Responsibility
Family Happiness	Security
Freedom	Self-respect
Friendship	Spirituality
Health	Wealth
Helpfulness	Wisdom
Inner Harmony	

Take no longer than 10 minutes and list all of the values above in order of importance to you. Rank them from 1 to 20 with 1 being the most important value to you.

eselling®

Are there any values that are missing on that list? If so, please feel free to add your own.

A definition of a value is something that you believe in and that is important to you. They usually have some sort of emotional involvement with you, too.

So, you've got your ranked list…

Now is this you?

Is this what you stand for and what is important to you?

You're starting to build your own personal brand!

What you Do

Some elements of what you do are easy to identify.

The sports you play, the books you enjoy reading and even the TV shows you watch are all simple activities that people can easily observe.

When you participate in a discussion forum, what you do is also reflected there in the way that you answer questions and even the questions that you choose to answer.

What you represent as a sales professional is also a reflection of what you do, though it may be less apparent to others and even to you.

Instead of thinking about what you sell, think about it in terms of what it does for the customer.

How does it help them?

Do you help them make their own products more efficiently?

Do you help them make better financial or process decisions?

If you help companies grow more food to feed the world, build safer cars, save money, spend less, or whatever it may be, focus on conveying that through your online presence.

To Do:

Instead of thinking in terms of "I sell Photocopier machines", reverse this by completing the following statement:

"I help (type of customer here) to ... ..."

So an example could be:

"I help small owners to cut through the fog and all of the conflicting information out there about copier machines so they can make a better-informed decision about their copier requirements that will ultimately result in reduced costs for them and a higher quality finish for their own printing"

Take 10 minutes and just write sentence after sentence until you nail the right statement.

Sometimes you can achieve this in just 1 or 2 rewrites.

How You Do It

Your style is a reflection of your values and round out your personal brand.

In this context, style is about how you do things.

Online, it's fairly easy to reflect your style through any of the types of content that you produce.

Remember that your personal brand is far more than just the packaging.

If your brand is radically altered because of a new haircut, your brand was weak to begin with.

Focus on revealing who you are and stand out boldly online.

That doesn't mean you have to have a loud and wild personality to succeed online.

Rather, it means that you need to be consistent with who you are and let it show through all you do online.

To Do:

What's your personal style?

What style do you want to be known for in the way that you position yourself online and in the way that you sell?

- Mr/Mrs Dependable?

- Champion of the (insert your type of customer here) industry?

- Edgy?

- Futurist?

- "Been there and done that"?

- Lighthearted?

SEAN MCPHEAT

Brainstorm this for 10 minutes.

Be true to yourself though, it's got to be you.

I don't think Gordon Ramsay could come across as a "pink and fluffy" boss no matter how hard he tried!

Let Your Online Personality Shine Through!

Turn on a talk radio station or listen to a podcast from a website like podomatic.com and you'll see something in common throughout the most popular shows.

You encounter distinctive personalities!

Some you may not care for. Perhaps the host is too aggressive, silly, passive, or hyper for your tastes.

They may have an ideology with which you do not agree.

On the other hand, you may find someone you simply click with from the very first listen to.

People who are willing to put their personality into their content end up with the most connected audiences.

Ironically, not all of these followers are fans, but they are paying attention!

One interesting example of this phenomenon is with the American Radio DJ Howard Stern.

When working for WNBC in New York City, it was found that people who highly disliked him listened to his show, on average, for longer periods of time than people who liked him a lot!

eselling®

Even his detractors wanted to hear what he had to say and kept coming back for more.

An aspect of your personality can be demonstrated through a persona.

Your online persona should fit your normal behaviour patterns, and reflect how others tend to see you.

Here are some examples:

- The instructive veteran

- The grizzled veteran

- The "I'm just a regular guy" guy

- The top-of-the-mountain guru

- The analyst

- The funny guy

- Ms Happy Go Lucky

- The Rookie or someone with a rookie's mindset (always learning and open)

- Archetypes from popular movies: "The One", "The Oracle", "The Architect" [The Matrix]

These are just a few examples of personas to give you an idea of how they can be used to help you create a consistent image online.

As you create a blog post, video, or even tweet, consider how that new content fits into the context of your persona.

SEAN MCPHEAT

There's more on personal branding in the **"Positioning The Maven"** chapter.

For now, complete these exercises and think about what your "Online Personality" is going to be.

Creating An Internet Footprint

It's hard to position yourself online with a single blog post or video.

One tweet will not turn you into a star on Twitter!

To be effective online, you must consciously build your online empire and leave a large virtual footprint. Your content should continually support your personal brand and should also create value for your target customers.

Your Internet footprint could be defined as how many times you have content or are referenced to online. It's your legacy!

A quick search in Yahoo for my name returns 47,000 indexed pages with my name on.

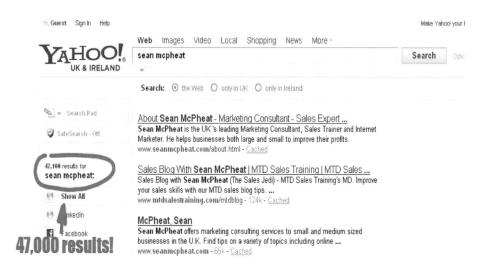

It's All About Content

There's a saying online that quality content is king.

Content, as it relates to you, is anything you create that can be found online. This includes articles, videos, blog posts, Twitter messages and even your comments and answers linked to that content. Every time you post or say something online you're leaving a breadcrumb trail leading back to you.

In reality, quality content is the name of the game.

Quality is defined by the value of the information to the person reading, watching or listening to it.

You don't need a slick production, just good info.

I've seen garage mechanics build loyal customers simply by shooting videos of how they work in the garage and sticking them up on YouTube. These videos weren't even edited but they provided great information that helped the customers feel confident about what was being done with their cars.

Before creating content, it's helpful to have an idea what people are looking for using search engines like Google, Bing and Yahoo.

This is known as keyword research (we've covered this earlier in "Understanding Your Space" and it gives you amazing insight into the marketplace by showing you what people are searching for online.

This keyword research will show you how many searches are happening over a period of time. Also, it will allow you to see what the competition is for particular search phrases. This combined information gives you a real edge.

You can find phrases to link to your new content. That will increase your chances of getting found and driving targeted traffic to your website.

Also, when it comes to content you will use this in the sales process too.

Remember our Commercial Estate Agent from earlier? He was sending video reviews of the properties out to interested prospects before meeting with them.

This makes him rise above all the other agents out there who simply meet with the prospect at the property and then just give them a tour.

For your own leads and prospects ask yourself this question:

What content can I send out to them before the sales encounter that:

A. Helps them

B. Positions me as an expert

C. No one else in my field is offering

D. All of the above!

Run A Blog Or Personal Website

Having your own blog or personal website gives you a sandbox where you can collect and share resources and information as well as your own personal vision and insights.

If you're also making videos or writing articles for other sites your personal blog gives you a central location where you can embed those other bits of content.

Setting up a blog is an easy process and it's also one where you can easily waste a lot of time on unimportant details.

The easiest way to get started is to open a free account at one the many free blogging sites available on the Internet.

Here's a short list of some of the popular ones.

- www.posterous.com

- www.wordpress.com

- www.tumblr.com

- www.blogger.com

- www.typepad.com

These sites provide you with some amazing capabilities and they are all free.

If you have a smart phone, or a digital camera, you can email photos to posterous.com where they will be added to a new blog post automatically.

New posts can also be promoted through Twitter and reposted on your Facebook page with no additional effort.

The kinds of information you share through your personal blog are reflective of the areas of interest and expertise readers expect you to have.

Of course none of this does you any good if no one can find it. Don't forget to put your full name in the title of your blog.

The search engines will associate your content with your name.

Corporate Blogs & Content Creation

Let's assume that your company has many functions, different departments and a level of complexity that makes handing out personal blogs and policing content quality a concern – so what then?

Well, the devil is in the detail and especially the roles and responsibilities of all concerned.

At times eselling® requires a team effort between Marketing and Sales where both teams need to "become one" to make it happen. Of course it all depends upon the structure of your company. The business rules, policies and procedures that it has will determine how eselling® will be implemented.

For example, if you are part of a large multinational you may have corporate standards that need to be adhered to, so you will need to liaise with the powers that be to agree on standards, style etc.

I'd recommend an initial meeting with the key stakeholders of the business where roles and responsibilities are clearly defined for all concerned.

Here are some of the key considerations that need to be taken into account in terms of blogs if your company is what I call "a complex one":

Are you going to have a central, company blog?

- If so, who will write content for it and how frequent will the posts be made?

- What content will be written? (Taken from keyword research from the chapter on "Understanding Your Space")

- Who signs off the content?

- Branding and style of the blog – formal and corporate? More personal touch to it?

- Who will you put down as the author of each piece of content? The company name? The MD? Various Directors? Business Unit Heads? The Sales Team members?

How will you set up the personal blogs?

- Will they be a subset of the centralised blog?

- What branding will they have?

- Do you want consistent photos of your sales people?

- Will the blogs be arranged by "industry type", for example, and then you have a "Retail Specialist" or a "Public Sector Specialist" who is the sales person responsible for that blog

- What can and can't your sales people write about?

- What topics and articles will they be responsible for from the keyword research?

- How much "personality" can they really put into their writing?

Please remember that eselling® is all about being different from the pack.

The last thing that you want is for your corporate rules to stifle your creativity, your speed to react to potential new business opportunities and your attempts to become more effective in your selling efforts!

That's the tail wagging the dog!

Don't think that eselling® is most effective with small- to medium-sized companies either. I have worked with multinationals who appreciate how important the eselling® approach is, and have worked out ways to generate content quickly, effectively and efficiently while still complying with the company standards and, at the same time, leaving room for individual personality to shine through from each sales person.

Contributing To Forums

Also mentioned in the chapter on "Understanding Your Space", contributing to forums and question and answer areas is a great way to demonstrate your expertise and to build up your exposure online.

Finding forums can be a little tricky depending on your particular market.

You may need to be creative in your searches but rest assured that people are having conversations about your types of products and services somewhere online.

To find relevant forums, visit Google and search for a subject keyword and the word "forum" or "discussion" after it.

Most forums will require you to register before you can answer any questions. As with any social media sites fill out your profile information completely as a demonstration that you are a real person and not a spammer.

Verified Account

Name Guy Kawasaki
Location Backyard fallvatar
Web http://alltop.com/
Bio Firehose that answers the
question: What's interesting?
Co-founder of Alltop.

There is no "standard profile".

All social media sites use them differently.

Apart from the obvious elements like your name and picture, seek out the area that lets you identify yourself to the rest of the community.

For example, a few lines in the Facebook bio area of your profile can add real value for those seeking to learn more about you.

Bio

As the first faculty member of http://gfydmember.com, I am thrilled to help small business owners extend their in-person networking efforts online, driving profitable traffic to their website. Social media training begins with learning how to use these websites and continues through a comprehensive social media strategy.

As a former tech teacher and social media enthusiast, I also help beginners become comfortable with their technology skills, and advanced users establish a presence online that stands out.

Directing the traffic flow online is fun. Translating offline networking skills into an online approach is powerful.

Forums and discussion areas will often have areas where you can introduce yourself as a new member.

Always take advantage of this. You will find that the most influential members of the forum monitor this area constantly. By announcing yourself as a new guest you can quickly build up a relationship with the people who can tell you exactly where the best sections are and even direct you to other sites that may fit your needs better.

eselling®

Another area that is an absolute goldmine for new contacts as well as for building your online presence, are the groups that you can join on LinkedIn.

You can create your own groups too.

In these groups you'll find discussions and questions on a wide variety of topics.

This is also a great place for you to ask questions. A well-phrased question will invite responses from other people in your field. Obviously these will be people that you want to add to your network. They may be potential customers as well. (I'll cover how to use these groups to hunt out prospects in the "Get Social" chapter.)

Have Your Own YouTube Channel

Simple devices like the very popular Flip Video camera, webcams built into laptops and an array of inexpensive video recording devices have led to an explosion of online video.

With over two billion videos being watched daily on YouTube you need to have your own presence on this website.

As you encounter questions through conversations with your own prospects and clients, or through your online activities, turn each question and answer into a simple online video.

Provide your answer in a simple, conversational and friendly tone. It's very easy to look "wooden" on video so just keep practising and you will find yourself easing into it.

YouTube videos can be embedded into your blog or website.

Do this with individual pages or create a compilation of videos by topic as you build your library.

Better yet, do it both ways. A secondary benefit of building an online video library is that TV and radio producers can find you and get a feel for what you would be like in an interview on their programme.

You might even get a movie deal!

Content Machine

Much of the eselling® model revolves around you building content and making it available online.

This content helps to position you as an expert and authority in your particular field and you can then use it in your prospecting and also for enabling potential clients to find you when they are surfing or doing research about available options.

It also aids in the softer elements of relationship building by allowing people to feel more of a connection with you, your personality, and to form a bond with you through your connection online.

If this last part seems a bit odd to you, keep in mind that great friendships have been formed through letter writing and pen pals over hundreds of years of history.

I have made some real solid connections with thousands of people around the world and some of them I have never even spoken to!

Just because you're doing these things through the Internet does not make you or any other person less real.

The Required Elements of Online Content

Effective content always meets one or more of the following criteria: it's either entertaining, educational, or enlightening.

I've even heard the term "Edutainment" bounded about on the Internet as a term that describes the best type of content in that it informs you and educates you, and at the same time is entertaining!

When people are seeking out your content online they're not going to sit through a 10-minute video that is not going to clearly satisfy one of those three requirements.

People are busy and attention spans are short. Don't fool yourself into thinking that your information is so important that it will override your viewer's or reader's inclination to click somewhere else.

Educational content shows a person how to solve a problem. It may also identify that the problem exists.

Entertaining content engages the mind.

To be entertaining you don't have to crack jokes or use special effects. A tour of a manufacturing floor can be entertaining because of the way it engages the mind and satisfies curiosity.

On the other hand, standing in front of a blank wall and speaking monotone into the camera is likely to turn off the viewer!

When content is enlightening it builds bridges between concepts and sparks ideas in the viewer.

Creating Content

Online content should be direct, engaging, to the point and personal.

These are the same characteristics of good email communications. To create any type of content, start with your keyword research to find a topic that reflects what people are already looking for online.

Next, imagine that a friend asked you the question or asked for clarification about a product feature or whatever it is you want to share. Write an email message as though it is to that friend. This isn't a sales letter. You're sharing value with a friend because that's what friends do.

You now have the basic structure for your content.

Many people find this process a great productivity boost too. While some agonise over writing an "article" or a "blog post" they find it easy to write an email to a friend when asked a direct question. Use this to your advantage and get what is in your head out of your head and onto your computer screen.

Develop a habit of writing at least one piece each day – it will be well worth it.

Don't forget that it's not essential that you write every piece personally but please remember that it's your name against it so make sure that it's a quality piece and written in your style.

Also, visit sites like LinkedIn.com and answers.yahoo.com, and look up questions people may have asked about topics in your field.

Write your own detailed answer using the technique above and store that in your content library as well.

eselling®

Options For Content

Now that you've covered basic information addressing keywords, topics and questions, start feeding that into larger pieces for distribution throughout the Internet.

When you create an article from a keyword phrase, for example, there's no need to cross that phrase off a list and never use it again. Repurpose that content so that it suits other mediums as well.

To further clarify repurposing content, let's first cover some options for the types of work you can create to establish your expertise and online authority.

- Articles

- Blog posts

- Press releases

- Forum contributions

- Magazine submissions

- Audio

- Video

For example, let's assume that you sell inventory control systems for large businesses.

You could start by writing a blog post about the future movements in the market place and you could provide links to other resources that would help the reader learn more about the subject (for example, books on Amazon.com, and videos from your YouTube channel).

Make sure that your blog post gets indexed by the search engines first and then you can use that content with some modifications elsewhere. (You don't want to "get done" by Google et al. for duplicate content and make sure that all of your articles, blogs, releases etc. are different in some way, i.e. they are not identical!)

You could also write an article (about 400–500 words) covering the same information.

This article would be used online through an article distribution site like EzineArticles.com

EzineArticles is a useful website because a lot of people not only use the site for learning and research but they are also looking for content for their own blogs and email newsletter lists too.

Write enough articles and you'll be classed as an expert author.

This looks very good in the search engines as your prospects and clients snoop around for further information about you.

EzineArticles is a very powerful site so you'll most likely show up in the search engines when a search for your name is made and hence you can showcase all of the information and knowledge that you've built up.

Sean McPheat - EzineArticles.com Expert Author
Sean McPheat is widely recognized as one of the leading authorities in internet marketing and sales. As a leading entrepreneur Sean has over 20 different ...
ezinearticles.com/?expert=Sean_McPheat - Cached - Similar

Next, you can write the content as a press release:

"John Smith Predicts All Inventory Control Systems To Be Outsourced By 2015"

Distributing your press release through an online news service such as PRWeb.com can give you a massive increase in online exposure literally overnight.

In addition to that, the various news forums, online newspapers and the hundreds of journalists that view your press release usually pick it up and use the information in any articles they are writing or indeed feature it on their own blog.

Take a look at this example below.

I published a press release about my latest sales research report "The Sales Person's Crisis" and distributed it through PRWeb on 27th September 2010 with the heading:

"Sales Industry In Crisis? New Report Reveals Even Bigger Threat Than The Economy"

By 25th November 2010 it had been indexed by Google on 3,280 sites. The release contained quotes from me, my thoughts on the sales industry, and the whole piece positions me as a thought leader within the industry.

Next, you can think about forum contributions. If you have found a forum that contains people from your market, keep an eye open for questions that relate to your content – you could even set up a Google alert to let you know when anyone online is talking about that subject and then you can go and "Enter The Conversation" with your ready made content. ;-)

Use the original text as the framework for your answer – a great shortcut – and tailor the answer to ensure that you're speaking directly to the person asking the question.

Don't take a shortcut here and just paste your content and let it suffice as an answer. People will be turned off if they get a feeling that you just copied and pasted an answer to them.

You can submit articles to offline magazines. A magazine article is usually between 1000–1500 words.

eselling®

Take the online article you wrote and expand the information to better fit the expectations of offline media. You can often use the shorter article as a "synopsis" to solicit submissions with magazine editors.

Do some research and build up a list of all of the trade publications within your industry and also any other magazines that would be interested in your type of content.

Build up a databank of this knowledge.

Submit your outlines to the editors via email and follow up with a phone call.

When you find someone that wants your full article, you can write the expanded version.

The beauty of this is when you get published in a magazine, by default, you are propelled into the "expert status" and you can use this as collateral before meeting with your prospects and clients. (We'll talk more about this in the chapter "Positioning The Maven".)

For video content, use a digital video camera or create a PowerPoint presentation to deliver the content as though you're having a conversation with the viewer.

With very few exceptions – and I can't think of any – no matter how "professional" you believe your audience to be, you should strive to appear relaxed in your video presence.

Online, your viewer lacks the benefit of a face-to-face connection.

Being "too stiff" on camera can appear almost cartoonish as everything seems to be magnified. Put your passion and personality into your delivery, but also relax. Skill comes through practice so don't wait until you're perfect before you let the world see you.

SEAN MCPHEAT

And finally, you can take any one of your articles or blog posts and then just read it out and record it as an MP3 and voilà – you've got an audio or podcast session!

This is the key to success:

Producing one piece of original content and repurposing it into several pieces of online positioning material and getting it "out there", which is what this next section is all about.

Promoting Your Content

As you distribute new content, let it be known.

Update the status on LinkedIn, Facebook and Twitter to announce to the world where you appeared.

Audience styles differ between the networks so tailor your message for maximum effect. With LinkedIn, the announcement can be strictly "informational" whereas Twitter and Facebook carries with it the context of greater personality.

For example, you might say that you're excited to be appearing in the latest issue of "XYZ Magazine" with your article on managing inventory systems. While this may seem like a minor point, it's a nuance that is subtly noticed through such networks.

Once you have content you need to distribute it so that it can be found.

For articles, add them to your blog. Create a free account on eZineArticles.com and submit your articles through their website.

There are hundreds of article directories that you can submit your content to.

Search Google for "Article Directories" and all will be revealed!

In my opinion eZineArticles.com is by far the best though and as I write this I've got 93 articles up at eZineArticles.com and they have generated over **72,000 views** and over **2,000 views** of my profile on that site.

Now that's positioning!

More to the point the content I have up at that site are blog articles I have already written so it took me just 5 minutes to post each article up there.

Now that's a good return for my time!

For even broader distribution, iSnare.com distributes articles through thousands of websites and mailing lists. There is a monthly fee for the service.

To distribute news releases, PRWeb.com, is the premier service for Internet distribution.

There is a small fee for each news release, but content submitted through this service will be up there directly in the major news portals all over the Internet.

For video distribution the "Heavyweight Champion Of The World" is obviously YouTube.com.

The maximum length of a video on YouTube is 15 minutes.

For maximum effect your videos should be about a third of this time, to take account of your viewers' limited attention span and available time!

When recording a video, be it live or a "show me video" using screen capture software, get to the point as quickly as possible.

Start the video by telling the viewer what you are going to cover, then provide the main content, and then summarise what you have covered.

Video viewers are fickle and will stop watching a video very quickly if they're uninterested in the content or confused about its point. Ensure the attention of your viewer by telling them right up front what they're going to gain by continuing to watch.

By using the free service TubeMogul.com you can share video content through dozens of other video sharing sites and you only have to upload the video once.

This service automates the process of uploading videos to multiple sites and provides you with statistics to give you an idea of which of your videos are being found and how often they are being seen through the different sites.

Creating regular content is essential for building an effective online presence.

As you expand your presence through social media, having a good sized library of quality content gives new prospects – and existing clients too – something to look through when they discover you online as well as when you have added them to your prospecting pipeline.

As you build your content, think of the bigger picture. What is a library of your information going to look like and what will it all convey to the people looking through what you have to share?

Get Social

What is Social Media and Social Networking?

Obviously, the idea of networking did not begin with the Internet!

Long before online access became widely available, people networked face-to-face at business functions, conferences, parties and other social events. The advent of the Internet took this networking to a whole new level, allowing people to maintain contact with others who lived in different cities and even different countries.

What began as single static web pages has become a web of interactive content generated by the people using the sites.

This is what social media is all about.

Media mogul Rupert Murdoch said it best, "People are no longer content to sit idle and be told what to think."

Word of mouth has always been of great benefit for a company (as long as it's positive that is!) and social media has taken this to a whole new level. In the early days of the web people used to email each other about interesting content or about the bad experiences that they had. Today, social media has given us the **"word-of-mouth grapevine on steroids!"**

Let's assume that I've sat down to eat in a restaurant. I lift up my knife and fork only to find a dead spider squashed on my pizza. I take a photo of it with my phone and I post it to my 4,400 Facebook friends, my 20,000 Twitter followers and the 1,000 LinkedIn connections I have saying something like:

"Yuk! Take a look at my Hawaiian Spider Pizza!" and then I link to the photo.

Within minutes my friends and colleagues can be tweeting it and posting it to their walls. Their friends then do the same who do the same who do the same…

A bad experience like that can become an Internet phenomenon if you're not careful!

While there are many different social networking sites out there, they all have some basic features in common. In general, people who sign up on a networking site immediately create an online profile. Profiles may include information on your home town, professional and educational background, relationship status, and religious beliefs. The profile picture further allows you to personalise your own page.

In addition to the profile page, all social networking sites allow you to connect with other users as "friends" or "fans".

The interactions consist of adding someone to your personal network as a friend and also through direct communication. Most sites have a way for you to post comments on your own page as well as your friends' profile pages for public view as well as an option for private communication similar to email.

While social networking may have begun as a way to keep in touch and reconnect with friends it has become much more than that and has evolved into big business! It is also a way to hunt out and become acquainted with prospects, to keep in touch with existing clients, to drive traffic to your websites and a way to position yourself and to build your personal brand.

A Brief History of Social Networking

If you say the words "social networking" today, most people think of Facebook or Twitter.

However, these were definitely not the first sites to take advantage of a growing online community. In fact, the first participants in social networking were those who were familiar with computer technology long before the PC became a common fixture in most households.

BBS or Bulletin Board Systems allowed people to interact through telephone lines and modems. People could discuss common interests or share files. Most of these interactions were between people who were familiar with technology and thus revolved around technology issues.

Although BBS remained a common tool into the 1990s, this next decade saw a growth of other tools. AOL's online system could be used to create profiles and search other people's profiles by interest. However, it wasn't until 1995 with the appearance of classmates.com that people began to experiment with launching websites where the networking component was the main objective. Classmates.com allowed people to register and then to search for old high school classmates.

Soon after classmates.com in the US and FriendsReunited.com in the UK, SixDegrees came on the scene. While SixDegrees was short-lived, the concept of social networking was here to stay.

Soon after that business folded, Friendster was created. Initially gaining traction through word of mouth, Friendster later had difficulty accommodating a surge of interest that resulted from mass media coverage. The site suffered from frequent technical problems and users were angered by the company's later attempt to delete and control profiles.

SEAN MCPHEAT

Many Friendster users later migrated to MySpace, a site that took off in no small part through the support of indie bands that created profiles to share information about themselves and their music. Fans also appreciated the opportunity to connect with their favourite bands. MySpace also expanded its reach to teenagers and young adults.

However, social networking wasn't only the domain of youth and musicians. In March 2003, LinkedIn was launched, proving that there was a market for professional networking online. LinkedIn seeks to connect people within and across industries who are interested in networking and professional collaboration.

Started in 2004, Facebook has now become one of the most popular sites on the Internet. At first, only college students could become members. In 2006, the company changed all restrictions to make it available to anyone who wanted to join. 2006 was also the year that Twitter began, initiating a successful experiment with social networking that focuses on users' status updates of 140 characters or less.

What Does It Mean?

With a seemingly bewildering array of social networking sites out there, you might not know where to start.

You may even find yourself asking, "Why bother?"

There are several answers to this question.

If you decided not to join a social network, you are missing out on an opportunity to connect with your friends. I know I don't want to feel left out if my friends are talking about something they saw on Facebook. Do you?

Even if you don't think you have any real-life friends on any social networking sites, you should still join the bandwagon because your potential prospects and leads are using this medium too.

And remember, a client is a stranger that you haven't met yet!

Thirdly, you can make some fantastic business relationships for joint venture and PR purposes too.

Next, there are many social networking groups and forums made up of the very prospects and leads that you want to attract.

Do you sell services to small business owners?

You do?

Well, there are hundreds of small business owner forums across LinkedIn and Facebook.

Go fishing where there are plenty of fish!

Listen in to the conversations and join in. Offer your pearls of wisdom, free articles and advice.

But go to give and not to get. That is a good rule of thumb that will put you in good stead in terms of social media.

So Why Use Social Media?

Years ago, having a website signalled to the world that you were part of the new online community.

Having a website made good sense too! People expected to see your web address on your business card. They expected to see an email address as a way of contacting you. When you networked with people these details showed that you wanted to connect with others. Having email and a website made it easy for your clients and prospects to find out about you and to reach out to you.

Today, social media has taken over what it means to be online.

With over 500 million people on Facebook, having a presence on there is like showing up to your neighbourhood BBQ party!

Not having a presence there is similar to snubbing that party! LinkedIn, Twitter, and other social media sites carry the same weight.

Social media is where people are focused.

Imagine the average family glued to the TV set in the 1960s. They trusted people on the TV because of their constant exposure. That exposure is a key factor in building trust. Major brand marketers know this fact still holds true today.

By connecting with others through social media, you are a "real person" and have the opportunity to build trust through the same repeated exposure that benefits the marketing efforts of major brands.

Social media also breaks down traditional geographical borders. It's easy to network your way to contacts in other countries without leaving your office.

Of course, networking isn't limited to new people. Social media is also being used to connect alumni, long-time colleagues and friends. By connecting through social media, it's easier than ever before to keep up with the goings on in your network and for them to keep up with you. Many of your connections are building their networks too. When you share your own valuable content through your online presence, someone in your network may know the perfect referral.

Keep in mind that, just like with networking in face-to-face settings, there's no true "auto pilot" operation that handles the networking for you.

Social media represents a toolbox and a venue for networking, creating and maintaining connections – but you still need to "show up" to make it work.

Debunking The Myths Of Social Media

There are a lot of misconceptions about social media.

Some people try it and then after a couple of months just give up on it without really understanding what the big picture of social media is all about.

Since I don't want you to be tempted to give up on social networking, let me address some of the common myths about it right now.

"You Have To Be Good With Computers And I'm Not"

Actually, most of the people on social networking sites have no background in computer technology.

Can you open your web browser?

Can you respond to your email?

If you can do these things, chances are that social networking will be a breeze.

Keep reading for the how-to's you'll need to get started.

"I Already Spend Hours On A Computer Each Day. The Last Thing I Need Is Another Online Time Waster"

If you're like me, you already spend hours a day at work in front of a computer.

Why would you want to spend even more time online just for the privilege of commenting on people's photos and updating them on your status?

Here's why: Regardless of the type of sales you conduct, real people are involved in the transaction.

Like you, these people are busy and view any change to the status quo as more work for them.

When faced with a purchasing decision, these people are likely to go to the web to find reasons to go with you or to ignore you completely.

Finding nothing about you is as much a reason not to work with you as finding something negative.

Also, chances are that if you've got an up-to-date mobile/cell phone then you can get applications for your favourite social media sites.

I complete about 90% of my Tweets, Facebook and LinkedIn updates from my iPhone so you're not tied to your computer to "join in".

I spend about 10 minutes using Facebook and Twitter each day and that's all the time you need to spend too. And I do this through my iPhone or iPad.

I also schedule time to prospect on LinkedIn as well. I schedule the time into my diary just as I would if I were making cold calls – more on how to use LinkedIn to prospect later.

"I Value My Privacy. Social Networking Could Violate That And Leave Me Exposed"

Privacy has become a major concern for people using online networking sites.

It is important that you understand the privacy settings for the sites that you use.

Most of them, including Facebook, have a way for you to restrict access to your profile information to only those people that you have already designated as your friends. You can also block people that you feel have been acting inappropriately toward you.

This way, no one will be able to find your private information. And if you still have concerns, then simply don't post anything that you feel uncomfortable with people knowing about. You don't have to add your birth date, home address, or phone numbers to your Facebook profile if you don't want to. Always exercise good judgement.

It's probably not a good idea to post pictures of your day trip to the seaside on a day when you've called in sick!

It's also worth noting that people can probably already find information about you online and this information could be exposing you to severe losses in business and reputation.

Have you ever tried Googling yourself or your business? Do it now.

Are you surprised at what you find?

SEAN MCPHEAT

Sites such as yelp.com are making it easier for customers to go online and share their opinions about local businesses. Why let one disgruntled customer dominate the web, when you have a powerful tool to fight back?

Use social networks to tell the story that you want people to hear.

Your First Steps With Social Media And Social Networking

Now that you understand the reasons to join online social networks and you've removed some of the mental barriers, it's time for you to get started.

Before talking about specific sites, let's cover some basic guidelines about social networking.

Each Site Is Different

First, each site IS different.

While some sites seem to have members from all walks of life and are thus more general in scope, others are more specialised and geared towards certain types of people.

A good example is LinkedIn.

A 16-year-old probably wouldn't want to join LinkedIn since it is set up to serve those in the workforce who are interested in connecting with other professionals.

Thus, it is always important to consider why you are joining a social network and whether a specific site will best serve your needs or not.

In addition to the scope of the site, you must consider the different formats.

For example, Twitter is different from Facebook.

On Facebook, you have a profile page with lots of space for information about you and your likes and dislikes.

On Twitter, you have a small profile space and only 140 characters or less for your status updates. If you are going to be effective on Twitter, you'll need to learn to make that limited social networking "property" count!

Basically, you want to be really clear about your motives in networking and then search for the sites and formats that will best suit your purpose.

This is a recipe for social networking success!

The Do's And Don'ts While Using Social Networking

To get you started on the right foot, here are some basic do's and don'ts to consider when stepping out into the social networking arena:

DO...

✓ fill out your profile completely

✓ be a real person

✓ use a photo of yourself

✓ create value with ALL you enjoy

- ✓ convey your personal brand by being distinctive, relevant and consistent

- ✓ make friends

- ✓ develop trust through authenticity

DON'T...

- ✗ do nothing but post links to the site where you sell things

- ✗ just be a commercial for your own products

- ✗ let yourself get sucked into discussions on religion and politics unless you're a glutton for punishment

- ✗ share pictures of yourself with comments about how drunk you were last night

- ✗ make statements which could get you sued

- ✗ be a wallflower

Top Social Media Blunders

Lacking Authenticity

You could also call this a lack of transparency.

Simply put, people expect to deal with real people.

Even Superman had bad days as evidenced every time a villain got their hands on a piece of Kryptonite or kidnapped one of his friends!

eselling®

These vulnerabilities are what make Superman accessible. Without these, there's nothing to relate to or to connect with.

By positioning yourself online as a facade of perfection, you leave yourself in the same situation. People don't see you as being real. You give off an air of being "too good to be true" and that turns them off.

This doesn't mean that you need to share every little woe in your life!

Rather, it means that you should seek to be real.

Even asking questions through your blog, Twitter or LinkedIn shows authenticity because it demonstrates that a. you're listening and b. you're admitting that you don't know everything!

Astroturfing

The holy grail of social media and your online presence/fame building is to get something you've created to "go viral".

When that happens, the message takes off as others share it and spread it on your behalf. Through sites like Digg or Twitter, a single piece of viral content can put you firmly on the map and make you into an Internet superstar!

Because of the potential upside of such a groundswell, it can seem alluring to have your staff or a group of friends, or even a virtual team hired from some far off country to simulate grassroots activity to make it appear that you've gone viral.

If you get caught, the backlash will spread further than your original message.

The practice of creating a fake grassroots campaign is known as astroturfing.

You might think that it's very hard to get caught doing this, but there are people out there who seem to have made it their life mission to investigate every viral success story to validate its authenticity!

Giving Your Responsibility Away

It's easy to assume that everyone under 30 at your organisation is somehow genetically imprinted with the ability to excel through social media.

However, they can't simulate your actual presence.

While outsourcing some tasks, like online searching/research and brand monitoring, can be effective, your presence is vital too.

More junior staff may not be able to properly convey the voice of your company.

If they're your only presence online, they will represent the face of your company to the outside world, so if you have to go down this route then make sure that you balance it with your presence (with more of you than them!)

Treating Your Activity Like A Rocket Launch

I have seen people agonise for hours about how to write a 140-character message for Twitter.

While you're wasting your time analysing your words to death, masters of social media are having conversations with your potential customers online.

Time passes quickly on the Internet so be sure to put action first.

Those who make no mistakes are not making a difference.

If you say something that turns out to be stupid just confess like a real person would and move forward. Give yourself permission to do things badly once in a while and join the ranks of the greatest geniuses in history!

Overdoing It

Services like Facebook offer the ability to "aggregate" content from other services to provide automatic updates for your account.

While this may seem like a very efficient thing to do, it's often not effective.

If your Facebook account is cluttered with all of your updates from Twitter, YouTube, Google Reader and your blog, your followers are likely to be inundated with it all.

This will lead to them squelching you out!

Followers that aren't listening are of no use to you.

Different social media sites have a different way of interacting.

Just as you "suss out the room" in a public meeting, seek to learn the lay of the land on different social media sites and tailor your approach accordingly.

Not Listening

Listening online involves monitoring your brand and listening to the trends and conversations that others are having online.

Note and understand what people are saying first and then talk back and talk with.

Listening through social media is too easy not to do it.

You can monitor key discussion phrases and keywords through Google and Twitter and let them deliver the results. Visit discussion forums where people are talking about the types of products or services you're offering.

Don't stop your listening efforts just with the names of your company and products.

Listen for the types of issues that affect your customers. Spot the trends and talk about them before they become news.

Quitting

Online activity is not "a campaign".

It's an active presence. Face it, the online world is just as real as interacting with people at the gym or at the office.

Treating social media activity as though it's an advertising run or a numbers game is a major mistake.

You're developing a new presence in a new landscape.

Social Networking Through Social Media

Networking through social media is really no different from networking in the midst of a cocktail party!

All kinds of people show up to such events.

Some will hide behind the punch bowl and speak with no one the entire night!

Others will find a person that they know and will be joined at the hip to them until home time!

And others deftly move into new conversations and seek to meet new people all night long.

To network effectively through social media, you must emulate the person who moves into new conversations and engages people.

It doesn't matter how many followers or fans you have on any social media network if you aren't engaging any of those people.

The other extreme can be detrimental as well. If you constantly barrage people with messages and links, they won't be able to keep up with it all.

You may not be blocked outright by others but people will tend to notice you less and less and will not be likely to take action when you ask them too.

Using Social Media To Build Your Online Presence

Everything that you do online contributes to your personal brand.

To understand a personal brand and its importance, let's consider the example we used earlier with regard to Coca-Cola.

While the ingredients are the same and the design of the can are the same each person has a different relationship with that can and its contents.

Some people love it. Some hate it. Some are indifferent.

The makers of Coca-Cola spend millions of dollars each year to present what they believe their brand to be, but in the end if you asked the opinions of 100 people you'd get a 100 different descriptions of each person's relationship with that brand.

So what can the company do about this?

The only real thing they can do is to maintain consistency and stick to their "ingredients". Enough people love Coca-Cola for it not to matter who doesn't.

Incidentally, if you want to know what can happen when you break the trust with your followers research "New Coke".

When that product was developed the company had taste test data providing that people actually preferred the taste of New Coke to Coca-Cola "Classic".

Shouldn't that have been enough of a reason to make a change?

Sadly not and the result was a huge marketing and public relations disaster!

The company seemed to have neglected the most important rule of branding and that's to maintain the trust of those who love you by being consistent.

eselling®

A personal brand is very similar. You're made up of different ingredients. You have roles (like being a mother/father, friend, coach), styles (energetic, loving, methodical, humorous) and skills (organising, coming up with ideas, being the peacemaker, negotiating, making connections).

When you fill out your social media profile, write articles and posts on your blogs, or make comments directed at other people, you should be aware enough of your personal brand ingredients to make sure you're following your formula.

If not, you're in danger of "New Coking" yourself!

The Social Media Model:

Using The Sales Funnel With Social Media

The sales funnel, which is a systematic approach to selling a product or service, works in basically the same way online as it does offline with one notable exception.

Your videos, tweets, blog posts and other forms of content can be found online 24/7. At any time, someone may encounter you and follow the trail you've left to find out more about you and what you have to offer.

Remember that you're leaving a trail for people to stumble across you. At the same time you'll also be prospecting online and using your content as part of your sales process to build up your personal brand.

Either way you'll be adding new prospects and followers to your sales funnel.

And remember; as you build content online don't make it an outright sales solicitation.

SEAN MCPHEAT

Seek to provide value to the reader and then follow this with a simple call to action to visit your blog/website/call you/email you for more information.

To increase the number of visitors, offer them something specific like a free whitepaper, a free e-book, audio or a video series.

Tell them exactly what they will get from the content you are offering them.

A simple solicitation to join your mailing list will not get many responses.

Offering something specific with clear value will increase your visitor traffic and it will help you to pre-qualify visitors because they're visiting based on the value you offer.

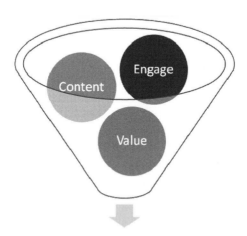

Trust and Authority

Listening: The Forgotten Benefit

While there are no guarantees of success in social media, or anything else come that, one thing can be found in common among all those who have experienced great success through the use of social media.

Social media winners listen and respond.

They engage directly with other people. They avoid the sort of online snobbery that screams "I'm too good to talk with commoners".

When GM set up a blog, it got off to a shaky start. The first posts read like a combination of a corporate newsletter and a marketing data sheet. Then, as the posts became more conversational and were aimed directly at the reader, the blog became a conduit for engaging the customers and fans directly.

The US cable company Comcast allowed one customer service director to seek out people on Twitter and respond to their complaints through Twitter in full public view. This bold experiment has landed mentions of the company on the front pages of the largest newspapers remaining in print. And the mentions on blogs, and even from other Twitter users, would easily count for a great deal more than the PR content produced directly by Comcast.

The deodorant brand Old Spice took a character from a popular TV commercial and put him into quickly made videos for YouTube where he responded directly to comments made about Old Spice on Twitter.

This video production marathon lasted for only two days but quickly became a top trend on Twitter and was mentioned constantly on multiple social media networks for days after.

While these examples may seem more "flashy" and consumer oriented than what you think may be needed for what you sell, consider the essential element of listening and think how you could apply it to your online activities.

Seek out conversations about products and services in your marketplace.

Look for discussions about your client's and prospect's products.

Your own personal brand is impacted by this model as well. You are defined as much by what you hear as what you say.

So we've covered why you need to use Social Media. Let's now look at three of the main social media sites (LinkedIn, Facebook & Twitter) and how to use them properly to create a stream of qualified prospects and to position yourself as the pre-eminent authority within your industry.

Social Media Services: LinkedIn

What Is It?

LinkedIn is a home to over 70 million professionals who are engaged in professional networking.

This site has a far more serious tone to it compared to sites like Twitter and Facebook. It's not exactly stuffy, but don't expect to find the more casually social features like picture sharing on this site.

If you're into Business 2 Business sales then LinkedIn provides you with a potential goldmine of leads and prospects ... if you know what you're doing that is!

Why Use It?

This site is where people go with the intended purpose of professional networking.

Here you'll find individuals from just about every industry as well as old classmates and work colleagues and special interest groups for alumni, businesses and special interests.

Networking with LinkedIn seems to be misunderstood by a large population of people. While it might make sense to limit your connections on Facebook only to "real friends", LinkedIn is a professional networking site.

When you meet someone face-to-face, do you reject their offer of a business card until you know them better? Doing so with contacts through LinkedIn is an equally odd behaviour.

The one area where you should use some prudence is with LinkedIn's ability to provide recommendations.

These recommendations carry your name and are linked to your profile as well.

If you put your name to an endorsement to someone you don't know, it can come back to haunt you if they turn out to be a consistently poor performer or a social media spammer for example!

If you're going to write a recommendation for someone, share your personal experiences working with that person and categorise your opinions about them from that context.

How Does LinkedIn Work?

LinkedIn follows the concept of "six degrees of separation".

According to this concept you are connected to any person on earth through no more than six levels of association. If you'd like to meet Richard Branson, there's a good chance that you know someone who knows someone who knows him.

Sometimes the connection is even more direct than that.

Using LinkedIn, you create connections with your 1st level of contacts. These are the people that you know. LinkedIn has the ability to scan your address books to help streamline this process.

As you meet new people, you can look them up on LinkedIn and invite them to join your network as long as you have their email address. The benefit of a new network connection is beneficial to both you and the person you add. They have access to a larger network of people and you do as well.

As with any social media site, joining is designed to be quite easy, otherwise you wouldn't find the tens of millions of people using LinkedIn for professional networking.

Simply, visit http://www.linkedin.com and click **Join Now** to get started.

The screen capture on page 165 is what the front page looked like at the time of writing. Most popular social media sites change and tweak their look on a regular basis so what you see on your screen may be slightly different but you should always find some form of "join now" on this and every social media site that you can join.

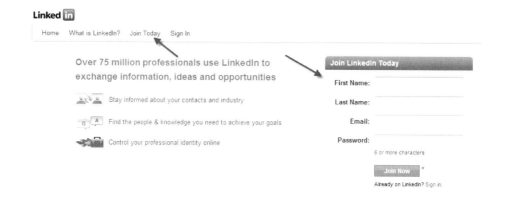

Your Profile

Your profile on LinkedIn is a little different from what you would expect to find on other social medial sites.

Here, your profile is focused almost entirely on the contents of your résumé and information that supports your professional development and current status.

LinkedIn also supports an option to display all or parts of your profile to the public.

Your public profile is very search engine friendly so take advantage of this opportunity to have another piece of virtual property pointing to you from the search engines.

Business startup expert Guy Kawasaki shows his original LinkedIn profile on a blog post at...

(http://blog.guykawasaki.com/2007/01/linkedin_profil.html)

...along with the commentary he received from one of LinkedIn's designers.

A partial screenshot of his original profile is below along with the comments made from Mike Lin.

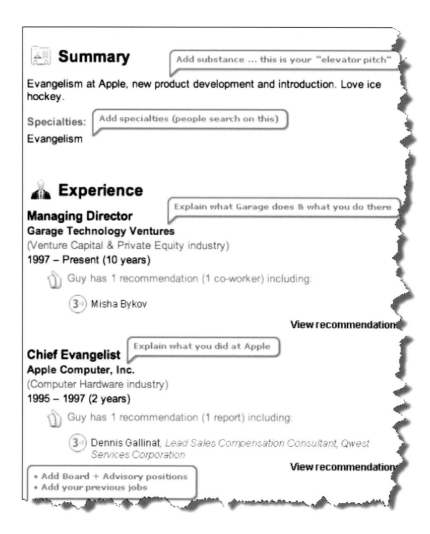

These comments – as seen in the screen capture above and at his blog post – are a great guideline as to how any profile should be constructed.

Even just comparing the summary portion of his new profile on page 167 to screen capture above, it's easy to see the substantial improvement.

eselling®

Guy Kawasaki's Summary

My personal mantra is "empower entrepreneurs." When all is said and done, I'm a marketing guy. I established my professional reputation as a software evangelist at Apple back in the 80s. Now I lead a peripatetic (peripathetic?) existence: blogger, venture capitalist, author, and speaker.

I am the author of eight books: The Art of the Start, Rules for Revolutionaries, How to Drive Your Competition Crazy, Selling the Dream, The Macintosh Way, Hindsights, Database 101, and The Computer Curmudgeon.

Guy Kawasaki's Specialties:

Marketing, evangelism, new-product introduction, keynote speeches, and wrist shots.

Essential Applications

In addition to the basic features offered by LinkedIn, a number of plug-in applications have been developed to integrate other popular services into your profile.

Please make use of these as they are what sets your profile apart from the others.

Here are some of the "must have" applications.

Link In Your Blog

There are a couple of applications that enable you to connect your blog into a portion of your profile.

Visitors to your profile will then be able to see the most recent posts to your blog and they can then visit your blog to read the full article.

These applications are very important for your LinkedIn positioning because as you create new content via your blog posts then your LinkedIn profile is updated accordingly.

Here's a screenshot of my own profile and what the application looks like to a viewer.

SlideShare

SlideShare is the best way to share presentations on LinkedIn!

You can upload and display your own presentations and documents which means that you can showcase information about your company, your industry, your products and services as well as information about yourself.

It's also very useful for educating your prospects and clients.

SlideShare is present on both Linkedin and Facebook.

Sync both these accounts with SlideShare and you have a holy triad. Upload to any one – SlideShare, Facebook or LinkedIn and it will show up instantly on all three.

Twitter

Similar to Facebook and Twitter, LinkedIn has its own status update area where you can share what you're up to with your network connections.

Using the Twitter application will automatically import new updates from your Twitter status to your LinkedIn status whenever you make a Tweet.

Whether you choose to use this or not is a matter of personal preference.

On one hand, this can be very efficient and can easily provide fresh new content to gain the notice of your contacts through LinkedIn.

On the other hand, depending on how you choose to use Twitter you may feel your Twitter content is a little too casual for your LinkedIn activity.

The Reading List By Amazon

You can extend your professional profile by sharing the books that you're reading with other LinkedIn members.

SEAN MCPHEAT

You can also find out what you should be reading by following updates from your connections, people in your field, or other LinkedIn members of professional interest to you.

It's an interesting application and you can soon find that others are following your reading list!

Summary

At the very least you should hook up your blog to your LinkedIn account.

There are many other applications that you can choose in addition to those that I have mentioned in this section.

Remember, you need to add value to the user experience so only use these applications if you are going to provide something useful to your connections.

Over-hyped sales material will not go down well!

Building Connections And Growing Your Network

LinkedIn is the perfect place for you to build your network as you meet new people.

By inviting people to join your network, you're putting the value of a new acquaintance to immediate use.

When you meet someone new, take their card and look them up on LinkedIn using the search capabilities.

You can do the same for existing clients and for anyone that enters your pipeline.

eselling®

In order to invite someone to connect with you on LinkedIn, you need to know their email address.

When you invite someone to join your network with LinkedIn, you will be given the opportunity to include a short message for the recipient.

Do not leave this as the default message.

The default message is illustrated below.

Invitations: Received   Which invitations should you accept?

Join my network on LinkedIn

    From: Sean [info]

    Date: October 15, 2009

      To: James Bond

  Status: Pending

Sean has indicated you are a **Friend**:

James,

I'd like to add you to my professional network on LinkedIn.

-Sean

A message like this looks spammy and impersonal and gives the impression that the sender is just sending out messages randomly.

So I'd recommend that you change the default message to include a short and concise invitation to your new contact inviting them to join your network with a reminder of where and how you met.

SEAN MCPHEAT

Join my network on LinkedIn

From: Sean info
Date: October 15, 2009
To: James Bond
Status: Pending

Sean has indicated you are a **Friend**:

Hi James,

I hope you are well?

We met at the Call Centre conference last Wednesday where we discussed automatic diallers.

It would be great to keep in touch as we may be able to help each other in the future.

Thanks again and talk soon

Sean

PS It's a shame our teams have just drawn each other in the cup! Up the Hammers!

Prospecting Using LinkedIn

I could write a whole book in itself on how to prospect using LinkedIn but within this section I'd like to cover some of the main ways that you can hit the ground running!

Using Network Introductions To Prospect

As any experienced networker can tell you, receiving an introduction from a mutual acquaintance can open windows of opportunity that otherwise would have taken a whole lot of time and effort to achieve.

Through LinkedIn you can gain access to your connections' connections via an introduction.

For example, if you find a valuable contact and that contact has a connection with one of your 1st Level connections (a 1st Level connection is someone who is directly connected to you) then you can request a network introduction in order to gain their person's contact info or a response.

You can find out who is connected to your connections in a couple of ways.

The easiest way is to go to the profile page of one of your 1st level connections and see if they allow you to look through their connections. So for the purposes of this exercise, let's assume that you are connected to me and you want to rifle through my connections to see if there is anyone who you would like an introduction to.

First, you'd go to my profile page and see if my connections are hidden or not.

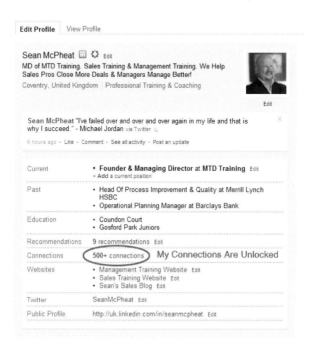

Whether you keep your connections hidden or open for all to see is an option in your settings panel. Your connections will always be able to see shared connections though.

If we've got shared connections, or the list is open, then the number of connections will look like a hyperlink in blue. You'll need to click on this to find out which option has been chosen.

So let's assume that my connections are unhidden. You will now have the opportunity to look through all my connections and make a list of the ones that you'd like to be connected with.

Now a word of warning here!

Don't expect me to introduce you to any of my connections if you don't network with me regularly and you are genuine.

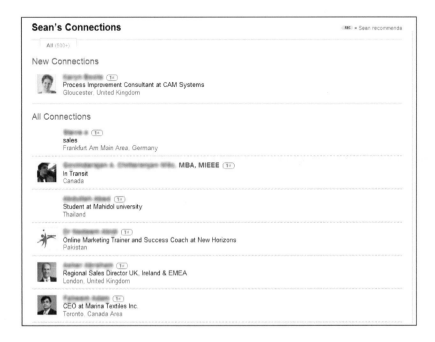

I've had people make a connection with me saying they are a fan of my work etc. only to ask me 2 days later to recommend them to some of the people in my list!

I know nothing about them!

So if you are going to go down the route of getting introductions from your 1st level connections then make sure that you "court" them first and provide value to them before asking whether you can add value to others.

So let's assume that I do know you and you want me to introduce you to "Mr Big" who is a connection of mine.

You'll first need to go to their profile page and then in the top right-hand side you will see this:

Click on the "Get introduced through a connection" link.

Once again, make the messages personal, to the point, and focus on what's in it for them.

Connecting to people you don't know through LinkedIn follows much the same strategy as any other type of deliberate networking. The advantage offered by LinkedIn is that you get hints about how you're connected to someone you want to meet – or you're told you're not connected to that person at all. When you make a request to get introduced to someone through an existing connection, don't send a giant story. Say why you want to connect to this person and ask for an introduction.

Now there is no guarantee that your desired contact will respond to your request, but it is a pretty amazing bit of automation which can literally connect you to millions of people around the globe.

Getting Introduced Through A Profile Forward

We've just covered how to "get introduced" through a connection. Now let's look at "profile forwarding" through a connection.

In the past I've made some great connections with Sales Directors and Managing Directors of organisations via this method.

Now if you've got a great relationship with an existing contact, then this can really open doors for you!

All you do is ask them to forward your profile to others.

Make sure that they are the people who will really add value to your network though.

For example, I asked a colleague whether he had any Sales Directors in his connections and he duly sent my profile to the 20 that he had!

Out of those 20, 8 of them became my connections.

So I became connected with 8 new Sales Directors within the space of 2 days.

Nice!

How long would it have taken me to have accomplished that via cold calling!

To forward on your profile your connection needs to go to your profile and then click on "forward this profile to a connection".

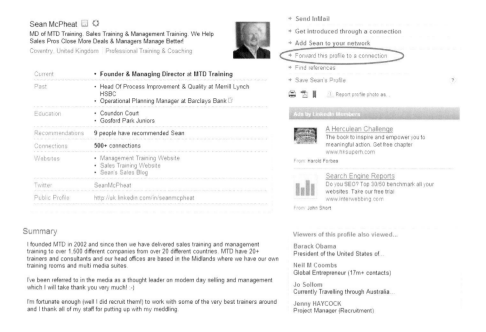

After your connection has clicked "forward this profile to a connection" they will have the opportunity to write some information about you in the screen below.

Once again please make sure that they send a personalised email and also include your email address so they can invite you easily.

Below I have forwarded James Bond's profile to John Smith. You can select multiple people if you wish.

SEAN MCPHEAT

Messages ▣	Invitations

Send Message   Cancel

To: John Smith   🖼

From: Sean McPheat<sean.mcpheat@mtdsalestraining.co ⌄

Subject: Sean McPheat has forwarded you James Bond's profile

Hi!

I've been connected to James for over 9 months now and he has really helped me with my management studies. He is such a giver and is an invaluable member of my network. I thought I'd recommend him to you too.

His email address is james.bond@007.com

Thanks again

Sean

Send Message   Cancel

☑ Allow recipients to see each other's names and email addresses
☐ Send me a copy

Using The Search Capabilities Of LinkedIn

There are several ways that you can prospect using the search functionality of LinkedIn.

I'm going to cover 2 of the most effective methods.

1.   What to do if connections are hidden from you

Now getting "introduced" via a connection is dependent upon you looking through the connections of their connections and asking to be introduced, which we have already covered, but what if all the connections are hidden?

eselling®

Well, one thing you can do is to perform an advanced search for the job titles or the companies that you are interested in and then see if any of your contacts have a connection with them. This is called a shared connection.

It may mean that you have to trawl through pages of results to do this.

Let's look at an example.

Let's assume that I want to make connections with Managing Directors of any industry. (Within the advanced search I can actually drill down further than just the title and include something like "Managing Directors" in the "Accounting" industry.)

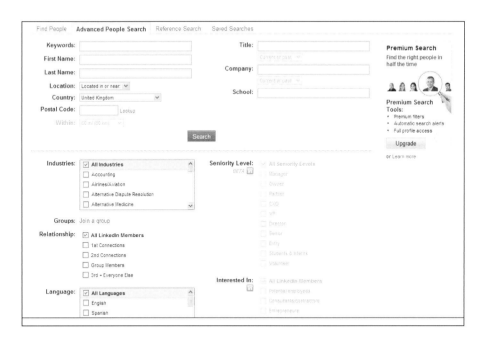

On the first page of results, I come across David who is a Managing Director and I can see that I have 1 shared connection with this person.

So by clicking on this link I can find out who it is:

It turns out that we are both connected to Robert. Now if I want to be introduced to David I will need to go through Robert first, which we've already covered.

2.   Using search and LinkedIn Groups to find "Mr Prospect"

By using the search facility you can search on the industries and job titles that you're interested in or you can just perform a search on the actual name if you know it. You can do a search on all three if you like along with lots of other criteria too!

Now these potential connections might be way down the ladder in terms of them being a friend of a friend of a friend of a friend!

So what now?

Well, the first thing that you should do is to find out what groups they are a member of and then go and join those groups. Find the profile of the person and then scroll down to the very bottom to see if they are a member of any groups.

For the example below, I searched for Managing Directors in the Accounting industry within 25 miles of my postcode!

I selected someone at random and here are the groups they belong to.

After joining some of the most relevant groups, take a look through the postings and discussions to see if the person you have selected has contributed anywhere and also see how active they are in the groups.

Below is an image of the group that I run on LinkedIn called "Practical Sales Tips".

This is its homepage.

If I want to see Chris's activity in the forum, all I need to do is to click on his photo and his recent activity will be revealed.

Chris's recent activity in the forum is shown below and you can then reply and join in!

You can also perform a search to see the activity of anyone else who is a member of this group.

Here's how:

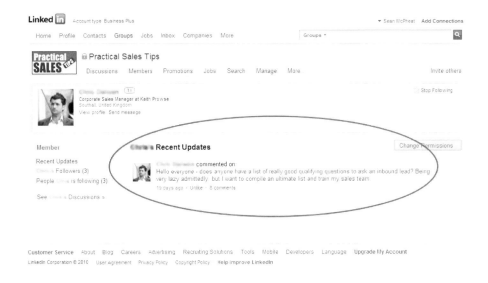

From the group's homepage, click on "Members".

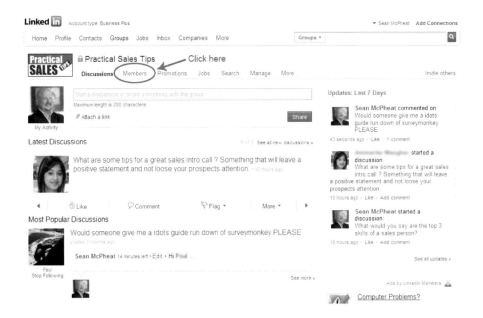

After clicking on "Members" you can enter the name of the person on the left-hand side.

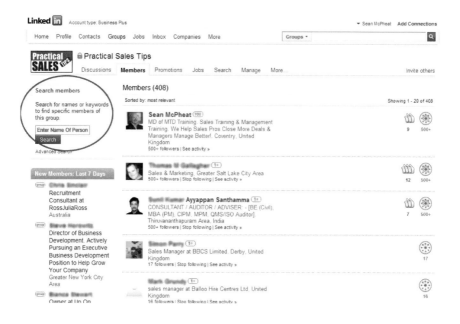

In the example below, I've searched for "Sean" and I've got two people in the Practical Sales Tips group who are called that name.

To see their activity in the group all you need to do is to click on "See activity"

If they have posted any discussions up or have replied to threads then reply to them and add value.

You can also start a discussion on the areas or topics that you feel they would be interested in contributing to. You're putting bait out here!

Become an active member of the group and start to raise your profile.

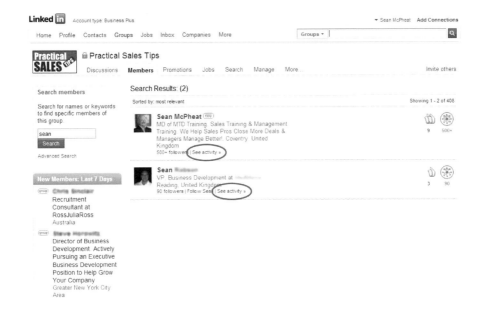

And remember; go there to give and not to get!

There will come a time when it's appropriate to make a move on the contact direct. Only you can judge when that will be.

The beauty of you both being members of the same group is that you can actually contact each other without having to know each other's email addresses. So you could say something like you're both members of the ABC group and you've enjoyed their postings etc. and it would be good to connect.

Searching Using The "Group Members" Filter Is Very Powerful

Once you have joined several groups you can then "go fishing" within those groups.

For example, you can perform a search for "Managing Directors" in any of the groups that you're also a member of!

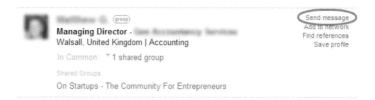

Once you get the search results you can email these people directly by clicking on the "send message".

A Word Of Warning When Putting All Of This Together

Please remember that as you build your credibility and network by using LinkedIn that this is not a spammer's tool so don't treat it as such.

LinkedIn is a vehicle for creating quality connections.

Don't expect to get any results if you don't network properly and build up your relationships gradually just as you would in the offline networking world.

You wouldn't dream of asking someone you've just met at a networking event for invitations to their network without building up your value to them first so don't do it in the online world!

Prospecting using LinkedIn is far easier and more worthwhile than cold calling so start to use it as a pro would!

Social Media Services: Facebook

What Is It?

Facebook began as a project at Harvard and has since grown into the largest social media site in the world. As of late July, 2010, the number of active users reached 500 million. If Facebook were a country it would have the third largest population in the world. These 500 million people use Facebook an average of 700 billion minutes per month. Whatever did we use to spend our time on before Facebook?!

The popularity of Facebook seems to be associated with the ease of its use.

People share messages, photos, videos, and play games with each other through an ever-growing array of applications developed solely for this platform.

Why Use It?

Facebook has become the premier site for millions of people worldwide.

Some people can't live without it!

Facebook has captured the eyes, the imagination and the attention of people that you probably know.

While the culture of the Facebook community may be very different from that of a site like LinkedIn, it is still a very active site for networking.

People on Facebook are a bit more interested to see that you have a real life but most people on there have jobs and careers too!

You may already be aware that a friend of yours sells property in your area, but if you see a message from them in your Facebook news, reminding you of that, will that influence your decision when you need an estate agent or when you're asked for a referral?

As a networking tool, Facebook is a great place to share information about yourself, and it's also a place to find an active, attentive audience too.

If you're under the impression that Facebook is a community of kids then think again!

All demographics are represented here and the most rapidly growing demographic group is women over the age of 55!

People of all ages are coming together and socialising through Facebook.

Getting Started

If you're one of the few without a Facebook account, getting started has been easy enough for 500 million other people so don't be afraid to jump right in. The registration form is found as you arrive at http://www.facebook.com.

After you sign up, Facebook will walk you through additional questions to fill in your profile. If you skip these questions, you can always modify your profile at a later time.

Elements Of A Winning Profile

An effective profile begins with your name and a picture. It is a violation of the terms of service to create an account using a false name or a business name.

Sign Up

It's free, and always will be.

First Name:	
Last Name:	
Your Email:	
Re-enter Email:	
New Password:	
I am:	Select Sex: ▼
Birthday:	Month: ▼ Day: ▼ Year: ▼
	Why do I need to provide this?
	Sign Up

Create a Page for a celebrity, band or business.

Facebook accounts are for real people.

You can create what is known as a Facebook fan page for your business, but your account and profile should be about you.
The picture you load into your profile should be of you and not a picture of your company logo.

Good pictures tend to be head shots.

If you recently climbed Mount Everest you can share that picture through the photo sharing capabilities of Facebook but it's less useful to make a profile picture of a gigantic mountain with a little dot of you standing at the summit.

Facebook also provides for areas where you can share information about yourself including a short bio, links to your websites and more personal information like your favourite books, movies and songs.

The more completely you fill out your profile the more of a signal you send out to others that you are a part of this online community. The reverse is true as well. A sparse amount of profile information and no picture sends a signal to other people that you are not actually there.

A great example of a winning profile that stands out is found with "The Queen of Facebook" Mari Smith.

She uses the bio information to clearly state why she's on Facebook and what she does to help others.

She also takes advantage of Facebook's ability to use a tall graphic as the profile pic to create a dominating presence and further showcase what she has to offer.

Do's And Don'ts

Your Facebook profile and the interactions you have with others provide a lens through which other people see you online.

So, as you begin to use Facebook, share pictures and updates about what is going on in your life and with your family, share links to news stories which are either professionally relevant or connected to your individual passions.

Never engage people as a group. It's not a group of people reading your status updates or looking at your pictures. Individual people are doing that. So if you ask a question or address people through Facebook do it as though it is a 1 to 1 interaction.

Don't post endless solicitations for business through your Facebook activities.

Once in a while letting people know that you're about to release a new product or service is a great way to generate buzz and excitement through the encouragement of your friends and connections. However, if the only activity other people see from you screams "buy my stuff" you will be mentally squelched and basically ignored.

Inviting People And Growing Your Network

Facebook provides you with several tools designed to help you find other people on the network that you may know.

You can scan your address book, and look at the list of friends of people already in your network. Each time you visit Facebook you can also see a couple suggestions for people you may know based on the information in your profile.

The more complete your profile, the more Facebook will have to go on when suggesting people to you that you may already know.

Using the search box at the top of the window, look for people you may know as well as subjects of interest. Facebook is a social network so be social. Make connections with people who share hobbies, associations and other interests.

It's really no different from making new connections and friends through networking groups.

When you find someone you may know, or would like to know, simply click **add a friend**.

As with LinkedIn, don't automatically assume that the person knows who you are.

Facebook gives you the ability to include a personal message with your friend invitation so please use it!

Searching For Prospects

Facebook does not overtly compete with the search engine giant Google and yet it offers a searchable repository of information on over 500 million people!

Perhaps you sell inventory management systems to retail chains.

Search for different types of products or store names to see what people come up in association with those words.

Yes, there is a bit of sorting and organising to do with the data but the results can be far more fruitful than digging through a phone book or Googling businesses at random.

The rich search capabilities of Facebook are also the reason for you to fill out your own profile completely.

A new connection made because of an association through a professional organisation or even a recreational pastime may be a big step towards your next major sale.

Listening Online

Communication through Facebook is a two-way street.

If you expect people to listen to you then you need to show signs that you're listening to them as well!

When you log on to Facebook you're presented with the news feed which shows content shared by other people in your network.

These are conversation starters so click on the comment button and leave a comment or you can "like" what they are saying too.

You can also invite conversations online by asking questions. To do this effectively you need to train your friends to expect questions and to enjoy the process. For example, polling people for an opinion and then not thanking people for their feedback, or interacting with individuals based on their answers, kills the momentum of the whole process.

SEAN MCPHEAT

Personal vs Business Use

A common question that I get asked about Facebook is whether or not it should be used for personal or business use and whether you should integrate the two.

As one sales professional to another I don't need to tell you that everyone is in sales.

It's a part of the lives of every living person.

I believe it is a worthwhile goal to live a balanced life and so it only makes sense to convey the same kind of balance through a social media site like Facebook.

In terms of my own Facebook usage, I have my blogs integrated onto my wall, I share photos of my holidays, the cars I buy, the places we've been to as a family, the conferences where I've given a keynotes presentation. I share sales tips, quotations on life and business, photos of my daughter's first day at school – you name it!

I want people to see me "uncovered" and to get an idea of Sean McPheat the person and not just Sean McPheat the business man. It makes me real!

Facebook Pages

One of the more recent features added by Facebook is the new Facebook page.

These can be created to promote an individual product, service, business or even a person. Facebook pages provide the means for a richer interaction that is possible through your personal profile. You can create custom pages using what is known as the Facebook markup language or FBML to display custom graphics and interactive multimedia.

In the same way that the activity on your personal profile pages shows up in your news feed, new content shared through Facebook pages also shows up in the news feed for any fan. This is a significant improvement over the old model of Facebook groups which did not share new content for the news feed of members. As long as your Facebook page remains fresh and has new content being shared through it all of your fans can see what is going on.

In the question of personal vs business use of Facebook, a Facebook page offers a more targeted tool intended for business and promotional use. Many people are still trying to work out how to make the best use of them!

It's unlikely that there is any one right answer so seek the best fit for your business. Some businesses find that it makes more sense to consolidate all activity around a single page while others have found that fan pages for individual products can generate very specific activity amongst their so-called fans.

Some stellar examples of this in the consumer product world are the fan pages for Coca-Cola and Skittles.

Each of their pages have millions of fans through Facebook and they have continued to encourage page activity and excitement by sharing related news and information through these fan pages.

Each time the makers of Skittles post a comment on their Facebook page, they receive thousands of "likes" and comments. From a brand marketing standpoint, this is solid gold because it's easy to see the activity and engagement of the community. An engaged community is paying attention and ultimately that leads to trust and sales.

SEAN MCPHEAT

As mentioned before, it's not about the numbers when it comes to fans and followers. Yes, if you represent a multinational consumer product you might be doing something wrong if you don't have millions of fans among the population of 500 million. However, if your market is a bit more selective, even a dozen fans can be useful if they're the right people.

How could you use a Facebook page for your business?

You could create pages for each product and invite clients to "like" the page. This way, when you use status messages to share news or ask questions, it will show in each person's "news feed" when they connect to Facebook.

To create your own page, visit http://www.facebook.com/pages/ and click **Create Page** at the top of the window.

As you follow the guided process for setting up a page, you'll notice that it's a lot like setting up a profile.

Facebook pages also support a variety of customisation options for special tabs and even content that welcomes first-time visitors.

Facebook page programming is well beyond the scope of this book and is something you should outsource anyway.

If you don't have anyone in your IT department who can set up Facebook pages, check your local résumés on craigslist.org or you can source highly skilled individuals from countries like the Philippines (http://manila.craigslist.com.ph) for only a few pounds.

Facebook Groups

Facebook also has a groups feature which used to be the only way to collect people together under a common theme or interest.

Today, Facebook recommends that pages be used for all commercial activity.

Using a Facebook group for anything other than alumni groups or other non-commercial interests may be a violation of the Facebook Terms of Service and subject to deletion without notice.

With such a huge population of users on Facebook, it makes a lot of sense to have a presence here.

Using Facebook – A Quick Summary

Keep in mind that people who use Facebook use it more for social networking and recreation than business networking per se.

However Facebook is still a good place to establish a presence and let people know what's going on in your life.

If your connections are on both LinkedIn and Facebook, then the Facebook elements of your communications need to be more centred around you as a person.

It's ok to share your photos, your opinions and your thoughts on the world but just make sure that they are consistent with who you are and your personal brand.

I use LinkedIn for the professional stuff and I use Facebook to portray my personality away from work.

Social Media Services: Twitter

What Is It?

Twitter is known as a microblogging service.

Compared to blogs, which can have individual posts totalling thousands of words, a single message on Twitter is no more than 140 characters. This restriction seems to confound every person who has ever used Twitter, but for those who stick to using the service, the magic makes itself known.

With over 150 million users, Twitter can connect you to a potential audience of millions of people around the world. These people are actively engaged in conversations about a wide variety of topics and few people stick to any one topic for long. That makes the Twitter community vibrant and active.

No single message on Twitter should be viewed as a conversation in itself. People who misunderstand Twitter tend to be fixated on the length of the messages and believe this constricts their ability to connect with others online. Here's an alternative view. Having only 140 characters for your message forces you to stop talking and creates an opportunity for others to be heard. Hopefully you'll take the time to listen.

Why Use It?

Twitter provides you with a simple platform for promoting all of the content you create online. You can share links to your Facebook pages, LinkedIn profile, blog posts, videos and everything else that you create. It also gives you the ability to connect with people in your industry and your marketplace. Producers and journalists monitor services like Twitter to find personalities for quotes and interviews too.

Twitter is also an amazing place to listen for groundswells of opinion and information. During the elections in Iran, women were sending updates from their mobile phones even though most other forms of Internet access had been blocked and the press weren't allowed near the polls. During the oil spill in the US Gulf Coast, people were sending messages, pictures and video through Twitter even though the press was being denied access to the scene. Even bad movies have had their opening weekends put to a halt as people were sending messages about the movie only moments after leaving the theatre.

While it's always possible that something new will come along, the fact is that today Twitter is like a direct conduit to the thoughts and feelings of people around the world.

They may even be talking about you and your company at this very moment!

Getting Started

To get started with Twitter, visit them at http://www.twitter.com and click **Sign Up**.

As always, take some time to fill out your profile before you continue. Twitter changes the look of their interface regularly, but you should see the same basic information as shown below. Unlike some social media sites, Twitter is designed around brevity.

There isn't a lot of profile information available so make it count. You can change it at any time so don't treat it like a moon launch.

Fill it in and adjust it later if necessary and as trends and styles change.

Elements Of A Winning Profile

Unlike some other sites we've explored, Twitter provides for a very minimalist account profile. However, you should still fill it out completely and include your photo as well.

One element of the profile is the "More Info URL".

While you may want this to go to your company home page, it makes more sense for it to serve as a stepping stone for people visiting your profile, so that they can find out even more about you. Point them to your blog or create a page that is specifically aimed to welcome people clicking from your Twitter profile. On this page, you can share more personal information, along with pointers to your other social media profiles and your business sites.

Do include basic keywords in your profile to help others find you.

If you're selling machinery, mention that in your profile. At least mention that machinery is among your interests to ensure you'll come up when someone enters that as a search phrase.

Do's and Don'ts

The most important thing to do with Twitter is to use it and to watch how others use it.

Don't just post "buy now" messages with links to your website. This screams to the world that you're just another spammer.

I was working with an acquaintance who had developed a low-cost video conferencing system that used webcams instead of expensive hardware.

He was looking for a market – unfortunately he waited until after developing the product to do this!

So I suggested that he do a search on Twitter and see what people were saying.

A search for "video conference" immediately resulted in a message from a person who said he was looking for a low-cost video conferencing service that was entirely PC based.

Talk about a golden opportunity!

My recommendation was that he send a reply to the person and suggest that he might have a possible solution.

Instead, my friend just sent a link to his sales page and told the person to buy his service.

According to the web logs, this person didn't even click the link and we later noticed that my friend had been blocked from sending further messages to this person!

What could have happened here?

How much further could this conversation have been taken with a more conversational message?

For example, "@person [here you insert @ followed by the user name of the person you're tweeting] I may have a solution for you. May I ask for more information about what you're looking for?"

This may have led to a back-and-forth exchange and might have led to a sale.

As it was, the doors were closed by someone who said that he was looking for the solution that my friend had developed!

Using Twitter For Market Research And Conversation Finding

Visit search.twitter.com to access an amazing array of information about conversations being held on a wide range of topics.

You can see what the current hot trends are too.

Many of these trends may be unrelated to your business, but an awareness of what's hot online can give you a feel for new ways to engage people in conversations and virally build up your own online presence.

You may notice that some words include a '#' character. These are known as hash tags and are used to help people follow conversations.

During the 2010 Soccer World Cup #FIFA, #ENG, #USA, #GER and others were used by fans during games.

There is no limit to what can be used as a hash tag. If you're holding a workshop, you can encourage participants to use a specific hash tag for their tweets so that others may follow and meet up online.

Other popular hash tags include #SXSW for the South by Southwest event, #Healthcare, which has been used for healthcare debate topics as well as by healthcare facilities to address the public, and #FF for "Follow Friday" where people recommend others to their Twitter network.

The possibilities for hash tags are literally infinite.

However, here are some which are very useful if you want to plug into the social media crowd, observe and gain followers of your own.

They are very popular but are US centric in their timing.

#blogchat is a weekly chat to help you improve your blog. It's live Mondays at 3.00 a.m. GMT.

#smbiz is a weekly chat for businesses of all types to discuss social media usage. It starts Wednesday at 3.00 a.m. GMT.

#brandchat discusses personal branding. It starts Wednesdays at 5.00 p.m. GMT.

Twitter is a lively and active service that has been shown to be enormously effective at building and supporting a strong personal brand. To use it effectively, you must use it to engage other people.

If you limit your activities to simple broadcasts of your sales offers and activities, your influence will be weak.

The secret to Twitter is to treat it like a party and step in to the middle of the crowd and mingle until you naturally connect with your ideal audience.

Social Media Services: YouTube

What Is It?

YouTube is a video sharing website through which you can share videos with a massive online community.

As of May, 2010, YouTube had reached over 2 billion daily views making it one of the top websites for online traffic. Owned by Google, YouTube videos also tend to get excellent search engine rankings if you place your keywords in the title and description field for each upload.

Creating videos for YouTube is a simple process. You can do it with less than £300 worth of equipment or you could simply use a webcam. Even newer smart phones now offer video cameras and integrated software for uploading video directly to YouTube.

Why Use It?

Video is very easy for people to digest.

Through a simple video, you can create a personal connection with your viewer while sharing information about issues in your industry, or even demonstrate your product and its uses.

A great example of a product demonstration comes from a series of videos called "Will it blend".

As chronicled in the book, Groundswell, written by two of Forrester Research's top analysts, a commercial blender company used small blocks of wood to test the quality of their blenders.

The blender would be run until the block of wood was reduced to sawdust.

One day, the head of marketing for the company made a simple video of this and shared it on YouTube. The video was not a commercial and made no reference to the sale of the blender.

The video became a hit and led to further videos where the blender would be used to pulverise everything from iPhones to butane lighters (which led to a large fireball!).

As these videos continued to proliferate, sales started to come in for the company from people who wanted such a powerful blender.

Getting Started

Now owned by Google, your YouTube account is connected to your free Google account. The process of bringing all of this together still seems to be in a migration stage, but it's at least as straightforward as other social media sites.

Visit http://www.youtube.com and click **Create Account**.

Your Profile

When filling out your profile for YouTube, add information on the types of videos you share through YouTube. This gives you an opportunity to declare your authority on the subject and also gives you a way to include extra mentions of your keywords.

Creating Videos

Not too many years ago, making videos for the Internet was a technical process that involved digitising video from a camcorder and importing it into your PC.

You then you had to edit the video and encode it to be shared on the Internet.

Today, there are products and tools available to make the process of video creation accessible to just about anyone. Videos are broadly categorised into two camps: Live video and show me video.

No matter what kind of video you create, end it with a simple request. Ask your viewer to rate your video, leave a comment and subscribe.

Live Video

Live videos are videos with you and/or other people on camera.

The settings for such videos can be in front of a whiteboard, on stage, sitting on a sofa or park bench or even from the shop floor.

Creative settings can make the video more interesting, but it's not important to over-think this and to get all "theatrical". A quick study of the most popular videos on YouTube shows that few are highly polished, slick productions. Online video is about content delivery so it is what you are showing and how it is helping the viewer that is the primary factor of importance.

Equipment for live video is inexpensive and you may already have what you need.

There are video cameras produced which are intended for exactly this use. The leading example is the Flip Video camera.

It doesn't take pictures or include any extra features.

It shoots video and stores it in its internal memory. When you're ready to share the video, you flip a switch to reveal a USB plug which enables you to connect the camera to your computer. Software automatically launches and guides you through the steps of choosing a video to upload to YouTube.

Many digital cameras also have the ability to shoot movies rather than still pictures.

To access the movies, you simply connect the camera to your PC or use a memory card reader and select the video to upload to YouTube.

If your PC has a webcam, you can use that too. For this, you may want to attach an external microphone because the built-in mics for webcams are often of a poor quality for video production.

When shooting live video, do spend a little time arranging your lights.

Overhead lights will not properly illuminate your face.

You can get the lighting right inexpensively with two lamps. Position each in front of you – one to the left and the other on the right – and light both sides of your face from the front.

Position one light at a bit more of an angle than the other, or position it a bit further from you.

This creates a slight shadow which makes you appear more "three dimensional".

In comparison, the lighting on your passport is flat and intended to be perfectly even. That's not the look you're going for.

Speaking on camera can take a bit of practice.

Your aim should be to speak conversationally, as though you're speaking to a person directly.

Show Me Video

A show me video is made from whatever you have displayed on your screen using screen capture software to record it all.

This could be a demonstration of your software or a web page. You can also turn PowerPoint presentations into video using free tools like JingProject.com or commercial software products like Camtasia and Screenflow.

These programs allow you to run through a presentation with a microphone and create a video as output.

If you already have a library of PowerPoint files for customer presentations then this is a quick option for generating content.

Show me videos can also be used to give prospects previews of key information without the need to wait for a scheduled meeting.

What Kinds Of Videos Can You Make?

Your options for making videos are endless. They don't require any fancy set-ups or editing.

In fact, highly polished videos often look poor online compared to more authentic videos that create a personal connection with the viewer.

Below are some ideas for creating videos which may fit your particular business.

The 10:10 Video Formula

This is the easiest model for getting videos created – and online – in the least amount of time.

The 10:10 formula is for two sets of 10 videos which can be used to blanket your niche with information about you and what you have to offer.

First, come up with 10 frequently asked questions about your products, services or issues impacting your clients in your industry.

Have someone start recording with your video camera, and ask you each question. Answer the question in a tone that is conversational and informative.

Imagine you're speaking with a friend over coffee.

The video is not a sales pitch. It's an answer to a question. Do one video for each of the questions.

Next, come up with 10 questions that someone might ask if they had no idea that the product or service you offer even existed.

These might be the questions you'd overhear at a restaurant or at a party. When you hear this question, you know that it's an opportunity to build a bridge between what the person is asking and the solution you have to offer. Again, this is not a sales pitch.

Just answer the question.

After completing this process, you will have 20 videos to upload to YouTube.

That's actually an impressive starting point compared to most YouTube accounts!

With a small amount of effort, you've positioned yourself as an online authority through content that should require you only a few hours to make.

Interviews

Similar to the 10:10 formula, have someone interview you, asking different questions about your products, service, company or marketplace.

Answer one question per video to build up a portfolio of online information.

YouTube videos are limited to 15 minutes and viewers seem to prefer videos with a maximum length of 5 minutes anyway.

You can also interview other people in the company about how manufacturing or design issues and all of the other elements that go behind creating and supporting what you have to sell.

Interviews of customers, detailing profiles, and case studies can also be of great value to viewers and can further position you as someone who is helping other people solve their problems through what you have to offer.

Product Demos

Can you demonstrate your product or service?

Can you do it in more than one way?

Most people might not think of a blender as providing a very interesting demonstration. Yet the amazing power of the blender featured on willitblend.com has attracted millions of viewers to watch it turn chunks of wood, glow sticks and even an iPhone into dust.

What you might consider a mundane demonstration may be exactly what your prospect is most interested in seeing.

A simple demonstration video can build trust through the application of the old adage "seeing is believing".

Presentations

Do you do client presentations, give keynote talks at conferences or speak in public?

Put a camera on a tripod and use a wireless microphone if you can to capture everything you do.

Edit these presentations into chunks and share them on YouTube.

Editing Videos

Your computer might come with free video editing software or you could purchase an inexpensive piece of software that will do the job perfectly well.

Learn how to use it and you can add short introductions to your videos as well as a screen at the end with text inviting the viewer to visit your website or to sign up to further tips.

Alternatively, you can outsource this work.

Your local University should be able to provide you with a selection of people with basic video editing skills. If not, check a website like www.elance.com or manila.craigslist.com.ph and hire someone to do it for you.

You could also edit the video yourself and hire someone to produce an introduction with music and fancy text which you can then include with each video.

Using video in your eselling® efforts easily represents one of the most effective strategies you can undertake online.

It lets people see who you are much more effectively than any other form of content.

For most people video is easy to consume.

Create a library of "background" videos for new prospects, which you can invite them to watch before a meeting.

Not only can they learn a lot but they will also get more of a feel for you and how you operate.

SEAN MCPHEAT

Listening For Leads

With all of this positioning and content creation please don't forget that you still need to conduct many of the same activities as you always have but you now have a venue where you can get connected to leads and prospects with greater ease.

You still need to keep your ears and eyes open and look for business opportunities.

You can "Listen For Leads" by:

- Loading up your Google Alerts system with key phrases that people would use when talking about your products and services

- Search the LinkedIn groups for threads and discussions

- Look for clues in blogs and forums

- Search Twitter for keywords, trends and conversations

- Search Facebook for fan pages and discussions

Case Study:
"How IBM Uncovered 'Millions Of Dollars' Worth Of Sales Leads With Social Media"

Below is a short case study of an interview conducted by eMarketer.

eMarketer interviewed Ed Linde II – whose team is responsible for building web assets to support the IBM.com sales channel and organic web visitors – about IBM's social media efforts and successes.

Below, Ed speaks about their Listening for Leads program, which he says has "uncovered millions of dollars worth of sales leads" so far, and is expected to grow even more.

Here's the interview. Read it, learn from it and think about how you can implement this into your own business.

eMarketer: How does social media marketing differ for B2B companies from B2C?

Ed Linde II: In B2C you're looking for a lot of interaction and collaboration between the individuals who tend to be a youthful audience and from time to time there's a celebrity element. In the B2B space, you want subject-matter experts who are known authorities on particular topics. They're credible experts on a particular area that people are trying to learn more about and make educated decisions on.

eMarketer: How are you deploying social media marketing?

Mr. Linde II: Within IBM we have a number of people in the brand areas who are blogging and doing things in the social media space relative to topics like cloud computing.

In B2B we have a number of websites that we built for our sales reps where we've enabled the reps to have a blog with RSS [Really Simple Syndication] feeds that are connected to LinkedIn and Twitter. Their customers can follow them where they have an individual relationship.

Some of our reps have Facebook pages also. We also have a program called **Listening for Leads**, where we have people we call "seekers" who on a voluntary basis go to particular social media sites where they listen to conversations and determine whether there's a potential sales opportunity.

eMarketer: What kinds of sites do the "seekers" go to?

SEAN MCPHEAT

Mr. Linde II: The "seekers" go on a voluntary basis to sites in the public sector. For example, government agency sites where RFPs [request for proposals] are posted, and there are discussions about proposals. In the tech space, there might be blogs or discussion boards about the new Intel chip for servers. We'll monitor those conversations.

Seekers listen to and look at conversations. For example, if someone says, "I'm looking to replace my old server" or "Does anyone have any recommendations on what kind of storage device will work in this in type of situation?" or "I'm about to issue a RFP; does anyone have a sample RFP I could work from?" Those are all pretty good clues that someone's about to buy something or start the buying process.

We try to identify those leads, get them to a lead development rep who is a telephone sales rep who has been trained to have a conversation with the lead to qualify and validate the opportunity. They'll qualify and validate it and then pass it to the appropriate sales resource to follow up.

eMarketer: How is IBM using Twitter?

Mr. Linde II: We promote our customer events on Twitter. When I say customer events, they could be webinars, podcasts, virtual trade shows or physical trade shows. We advertise some of our promotions via Twitter. And our individual reps use Twitter to keep their customers updated about interesting news, events and things of that nature. Each rep has their own Twitter account. We also have the handle @IBMpcs because we sell refurbished PCs.

eMarketer: What successes have you had with social media?

Mr. Linde II: I would say Listening for Leads has been our best initiative so far. We have uncovered millions of dollars worth of sales leads through our intelligent listening program and we've closed a lot of business and we expect to do more. That's going to be a big growth area.

The thing you have to be careful with in social media is you can't take your expert, for example, the guru of cloud computing, and expect him or her to also try to be a salesperson. Most people go to these sites and want the expert to be like a professor and to be as unbiased and antiseptic as possible. They don't want to be sold to on those sites.

Smart marketers use the expert to establish credibility, to get the conversation going and so forth. And then maybe you can have the expert point people back to the website where you can do the promotional stuff and the selling activity. By the same token, you listen for activity and if it looks like there are opportunities, you pursue them.

eMarketer: Can you offer an example?

Mr. Linde II: Let's say there's a big industry for used tires. You would go out to the places where people talk about used tires and listen for conversations where someone's looking to buy used tires. You would contact that person, interact with them and suggest that you might be able to help. You sort of qualify them and then hand them off to the lead development rep.

eMarketer: Is there some secret sauce that makes this type of program successful, or is it more that you've been able to identify the key places where people are talking about the IBM products and services?

Mr. Linde II: The key thing to making this successful is knowing what the right keywords are so that you can sort of search the various blogs and other venues where people are talking about your products. You need to use tools with Google that filter the conversations that are happening within blogs or on Twitter.

SEAN MCPHEAT

Typically, on the seeking side, we get people from the business unit to spend a couple of hours a week doing it. So if you have enough people doing that you can uncover enough opportunities for the lead development reps to follow up on. I can't divulge the number of people doing the seeking; it's a decent number, but it's not their full-time job.

eMarketer: How are you tracking and measuring your social initiatives? You mentioned that you've identified millions of sales leads.

Mr. Linde II: We measure against number of sales leads identified. And we rate the lead value from those leads. Then the win revenue and win rate. So there are four key metrics – number of leads created, lead value, win revenue and win rate.

(Thanks to eMarketer for that case study)

It's interesting to read how a corporate giant like IBM is embracing this approach.

So once a lead is identified how is it now managed?

Is there a different way to manage the "modern day pipeline"?

The Traditional Method Of Pipeline Management

In the traditional world of sales, you start with prospecting, you set up an appointment, get a meeting, make a proposal and then play the game of back and forth – I liken it to a tennis match – until you finally close the deal.

Depending on the typical sales cycle for your product combined with client business factors over which you have no control, this could take days, weeks, months or even years!

Meanwhile, you're forced to do a lot of work to keep the opportunity warm and you risk triggering the "pest alarm" and being squelched out of your prospect's mind.

Modern Pipeline Management

Pipeline management in the modern age is aided by your online presence and through your ability to keep in touch through automated means, blogs, social networks et al.

By the time of your first meeting your prospect has been able to review a lot of information about your solutions and also about you. You go into the meeting with greater authority and that allows you to spend more time working directly with the customer on solving their problems.

After identifying a lead and an opportunity online you should treat them exactly in the same way as you would any other lead and immediately add them to your CRM (Customer Relationship Management) system.

If your company is using a CRM tool you may already have the technology available to drip feed follow-up messages to your prospects via email and offline media. As with any other type of content this information should be of value to the needs of your prospect.

You should also add new prospects to your Social Media Networks too.

Invite them to your LinkedIn network and let them know about your blog, video channel and other sources of content that will be useful for them and their business needs.

Enter The Conversation

"Enter The Conversation" means getting involved!

It's about getting involved with your LinkedIn groups, updating you profiles, commenting on other people's statuses and questions, forums, blogs – you name it!

It's all about contribution. It's about contributing content, it's about contributing answers to solve people's problems and it's about contributing and entering the conversation when you identify a lead.

Just as with face-to-face networking, it's important to be a part of the online community as opposed to simply talking at them.

In the early days of the web it was possible to simply act as an online billboard, broadcasting your message with no regard for feedback or input from your audience.

Today, people are not content to sit around and be told what to think.

They want to interact.

If you're not willing to engage others about what it is that you do then your leads, prospects and clients will find someone else to talk to instead.

A Tale Of Two Sales People

Imagine, if you will, how the impact of the Internet and eselling® is changing the face of professional development and sales throughout all industries.

eselling®

One example comes from my own experience with a colleague in the construction industry.

He was a Business Development Manager and did not have an individual blog or website. A search for his name in Google revealed almost nothing. From his point of view, this was perfectly fine. He firmly believed that his industry was not affected by the Internet and there was no need for him to build an online presence.

He did not get involved at all.

Sadly, and unbeknown to him for some time, the search for his name through Google did yield one result.

His name was referenced via a 98-page PDF file on the server of a law firm.

That PDF was the court complaint for a lawsuit.

While he wasn't being sued, his name was listed in the body of the document.

As there was no other content on the Internet with his name, this one document was the number one, and only, result from a Google search.

As there was no legal reason for this document to be removed it remained at the top of the Google search results page for his name for some time.

Yes, the clients and even his own suppliers began to notice.

This simple document – which no one seemed to read well enough to see that he was not being sued but was simply mentioned – caused a real business impact.

SEAN MCPHEAT

Contrast that story with this...

Another colleague comes up in Google over 5,500 times.

Picture and video searches also show him repeatedly.

He's offering advice, sharing thoughts and visions and can be seen engaging the community through the activities and local events he supports. When you Google him, you get a clear sense of the energy he brings to the table and the types of subjects in which he's clearly an expert.

Based on press releases mentioning – and positioning – him in his field, he's received regular press enquiries to be interviewed or to provide quotes for stories.

You can find this person contributing content through a variety of online networks.

He comments on videos, is an active reviewer of businesses in his local city and is even a guest author on other popular blogs.

Building a strong online presence doesn't happen overnight. As with face-to-face network building, the next step is about the next step, not the next 1,000 steps.

Instead of worrying about having everything look perfect before you set out, simply take a step.

No skill is developed by sitting around and thinking about it.

You must get on the bike and push off if you are to ever develop the skills necessary to ride.

So get involved and start to enter the conversation!

eselling®

Positioning The Maven

Ever heard of the term "Maven?"

To be honest I had never heard of it until a radio interviewer called me one!

Let's go to good old Wikipedia for a definition:

"A **maven** is a trusted expert in a particular field, who seeks to pass knowledge on to others. The word maven comes from the Hebrew, via Yiddish, and means one who understands, based on an accumulation of knowledge."

Wow!

I like that term a lot because it is exactly what you are setting out to achieve via eselling®.

Three phrases stand out in that definition for me:

"Trusted Expert"

"Seeks To Pass Knowledge To Others"

"One Who Understands"

Those key phrases nail what eselling® is all about.

Effective sales outcomes are often determined by how you're positioned before you even show up at the meeting.

If you can position yourself as a "Maven" before you even show up then it gives you an immediate advantage over the competition.

Knowing that people are probably looking for you online anyway, why not make it easy for them and package what you'd like them to know about you into a convenient wrapper!

This is the "mother" of all pre-sells!

By sending your prospect some pre-meeting positioning collateral, if done correctly, you can turn up and they'll view you as an expert rather than a sales person before you even open your mouth.

Before visiting a new prospect for the first time you can further establish your position and authority with what I call **"the one pager"**.

This is a summary of how you help people, what you've done in the past, and it should also include elements of the online profile that you've built up.

It can help give your prospects an additional sense of comfort about meeting with you and it can also save them the hassle of searching for you online by showing them all the highlights that they should find there anyhow.

"The one pager" helps to pre-position you in the eyes of the meeting attendees.

It positions you ahead of your competition by presenting a roadmap of the value you've created already and the recognition you've received for it.

In short, it makes you stand out.

Here's a brief list of the types of things you can mention in your one pager.

- Bio and work experience

- Association memberships

- Certifications

- Media appearances

- Web addresses for article sites, YouTube channel, etc.

- Unique contributions to the industry

- A personal mission statement

On page 226 and 227 is an example of a one pager that I have used in the past.

So ok, it's two pages!

But you understand where I am coming from here!

The one pager is not a résumé or CV though you may find some minor overlaps between them. Instead, it is a document that highlights you in terms of how you help your prospects solve their problems and issues.

The above includes some media photos of me on the television including CNN and the BBC. It includes a front cover feature that a major business magazine did on me. I also talk about the awards I've won, how I am a judge for the "Young Enterprise" initiative in the UK and I talk about the work that I have completed for similar clients.

Sean McPheat

Managing Director

Founder and MD of international sales training firm MTD Sales Training, Sean McPheat has been referred to in the media as a thought leader within the sales improvement industry.

MTD have delivered training, coaching and consultancy to over 1500 different organisations and 25,000+ staff from 23 different countries.

Sean leads a team of 25 of the most effective sales trainers in the world and has appeared on TV on several occasions as an expert in the field of sales development.

Being a finalist in the **2007 British Business Awards** for his Entrepreneurial achievements, Sean knows what makes businesses successful. He was featured in the 2009 Who's Who of Britain's Business Elite and since 2008 he has been a regular judge for the UK's Young Enterprise Programme but was not as horrible as Simon Cowell (well almost!)

Sean has been featured on **CNN International, the BBC, ITV, The Guardian, Arena Magazine, Marketing Weekly, The Hong Kong HR Journal** and radio stations such as BBC WM, Insight Radio and LBC (London's Big Conversation) and has **over 250 other media credits** to his name.

Sean is the author of the **"The Sales Person's Crisis"** which has been downloaded over 20,000 times on the internet at **http://www.salescrisis.com** and he has a **Sales CD Programme** out on the market called "Drive Time Sales Strategies – 39 Practical "HOW TO" Sales Tips While You're On The Way To The Sale" **http://www.drivetimesales.com**

Sean is also a much sought after media figure and motivational speaker on all topics related to sales, business improvement and entrepreneurialism.

Having built MTD Training from a bank balance of zero he's living proof that with hard work and the right strategy anything is possible!

Sean's weekly email tips go out to over **60,000 people** interested in sales and management and he's a big player in the internet marketing scene.

Sean's blog http://www.mtdsalesblog.com is visited by **5,000 people** each week.

Delivering Sales Results In Partnership...

"**Delivers.** That is the one word that sums up Sean McPheat and MTD. On time, beyond expectations, at short notice and without fail. Challenging our thinking and working as a business partner who wants our business to succeed. Someone you can bounce ideas around with and who isn't afraid to give ideas and suggestions."

"Partnering with MTD is just that – **a partnership**. We view Sean and MTD as part of our business and not as a third party supplier. Our problems become Sean's problems and I am just so happy that he's on our side and not on our competitors!"

Contact
Email   sean.mcpheat@mtdsalestraining.com
Switchboard 0800 849 6732

Compare that to someone who just turns up on the day as my "competition" and you can see what positioning is all about.

Don't worry if you have not been on TV or if you don't have a long line of media credits, you can use your online presence to provide you with the ammunition for you own "one pager".

SEAN MCPHEAT

Let's look at an example.

Let's go back to our Photocopier Machine sales executive. His one pager could include something like:

"James has been providing printing solutions to small businesses for the last 10 years where he has saved his clients an estimated £2 million worth of printing costs. James has been featured on the web's no.1 Small Business forum website XYZ.COM and also hosts his own monthly video blog where he showcases the latest photocopying models – "warts and all!"

James has provided solutions to the likes of BIG COMPANY NAME, BIG COMPANY NAME, MEDIUM COMPANY NAME, SAME INDUSTRY COMPANY NAME AS PROSPECT and he has also published and written "The Small Business Owners Guide To Not Getting Ripped Off With Printing Costs".

So you can see even from the short excerpt above that James has risen above the status of just a printer supplier to a person that knows his stuff!

The published book was an ebook online and he strategically contributes content to some of the big hitting Small Business online community websites and forums.

Now that's positioning!

You As The Trusted Advisor

As mentioned before, positioning yourself online involves building a large Internet footprint.

This helps to demonstrate you as an authority in your field.

Using the keyword research tools explained earlier, write articles and blog posts, or create simple videos with your webcam, to provide information on how to choose the right products and services.

Go a step further and explain different ways to use the products or share innovative strategies that might be on the horizon.

Be a thought leader and talk about the trends and how new solutions may help businesses with their own missions.

The mission is to get found in as many places as you can and to use your online presence for materials and positioning offline too.

Even repurposing content through multiple forms of media can help you to connect with different audiences.

Not everyone wants to read from a blog or watch a video.

Taking the same content and using it in two different formats enhances your reach without having to produce additional content.

Start with a blog, write some articles and post them on various websites and then create some videos for YouTube as well.

As you position yourself in these areas, expand to new venues. Seek out magazines, newspapers and even TV and radio stations as places where you can provide further content. Even though the sun seems to be setting on major media outlets, getting into print or on TV is still viewed as a major plus by the public.

Visit blogs by other thought leaders in your field and comment on their posts.

Do not use this as an opportunity to talk about yourself and how great you are.

SEAN MCPHEAT

This will have the opposite effect you're looking for. Put your ego in a box and write a thoughtful response to the blog post. Relate to it. Suggest other views or reinforce it with your own experiences. This is a great way to become a part of the online community and your engagement can lead to your own blog getting more comments and being referenced by others.

You can also approach other blogs and offer to submit content as a guest blogger.

Blog owners are always looking for new content and by submitting content as a guest blogger you're helping them out and you're also increasing the value of your own online presence.

People don't know how you ended up as a guest blogger and the natural assumption is that you were asked to do it by the blog owner. The assumption here is that your knowledge and insight is in demand.

As a guest blogger, you also drive traffic back to your own website so guest blogging is a great source of free traffic as well.

Pre-Meeting Activities

Before heading to a meeting, or as you build relationships with new prospects and your existing clients, there are simple ways that you can add value while simultaneously enhancing your own authority and personal brand.

Forwarding useful articles and resources to a prospect or client is an age-old practice known by all the top sales professionals.

With the advent of the Internet the process for doing this is much easier.

Using the techniques outlined in the "Understanding Your Space" chapter, you're looking for materials and resources that directly relate to the kind of problems and challenges faced by your prospects and clients.

Forward these materials through email with a note pointing out the relevance of what you're sending.

Don't just blindly send a link to someone – they'll have no idea what it is and will probably be too busy to bother looking.

However if you get their attention by telling them why it's a useful resource, they're not only likely to look but they will associate you with that useful source of information.

Of course it's easy to go too far with this approach as well.

If you forward every little scrap of information that comes your way, what value do you provide?

Part of the value in the relationship with your prospect, or client, lies in your ability to be a filter as well as a guide.

If you do happen to find a bonanza of information that you just can't wait to share arrange the information into groups and consider sharing it as a compilation through your website.

Some of the materials you collect can even make for great blog posts, articles and videos.

Of course you should never plagiarise someone else's content but you can write your own blog post that puts your own spin on the topic, and reference people to other web pages for additional information.

Some people view listing links to other websites as being a counter intuitive strategy in developing a strong online position and in retaining visitors. However time and time again this has been proven to be a very effective strategy.

No one is going to believe that you are the exclusive authority on any subject!

By listing links and resources that point to other websites you demonstrate that confidence and poise of a professional who places the needs of the client in front of his or her ego.

Positioning Yourself For Online Authority

With the knowledge that your prospects and clients are going to search for your name from time to time, it's important that you can be found.

This means that you need to be generating content in the right places as well as ensuring that the content can be found through a search query.

Below are some tactics and strategies that you should consider to help you to build a strong online presence and to ensure that it gets found by the right people.

Positioning Your Brand

Positioning your brand online means building content and your persona.

Your content puts you out there and exposes you to more people. If you're just getting started, you may have a very small assortment for people to discover, but the beauty of the Internet is that what you do, sticks around.

eselling®

A year from now you may have 100s of blog posts, videos, and pictures. As you remain focused on your field, the incoming contacts increase.

Reporters and producers from traditional media now look to the Internet to find the influencers and the experts. They can see you in action through the content you're sharing and gauge how well you'll fit in front of their audience.

One great recent example of online positioning through content generation can be seen with the Old Spice brand.

During the winter, they developed a short add starring a former American Football player. It generated a lot of buzz throughout the Internet for its creativity and light-hearted approach.

In the summer the producers took the original star and began to churn out video responses to the continued chatter on social media sites like Twitter and Facebook. These videos were produced very quickly and several dozen where posted on YouTube over a two-day period.

While the market of Old Spice is quite broad, there's no reason why you can't duplicate the model of success displayed here. Old Spice listened to what was being said and responded quickly. How could you do the same thing? Listen to the conversations online and use them to create blog posts, videos and audio clips.

This approach can create a quick buzz and don't forget everything you create remains online for people to find. Build an event around your online activities and have some fun.

Personal Branding: From Product Vendor To Trusted Advisor

As a sales professional, a strong personal brand can have a very positive impact on the relationships you form with your existing clients and new prospects.

Keep in mind that personal branding is not just about image management. Focus only on the superficial and you will only have superficial results!

The relationship between how you're currently positioned is illustrated through the diagram below.

This relationship builds through both familiarity and through your successful efforts at developing your presence online.

Product Vendor

At the most basic, your prospect views you as the stereotypical sales person.

You identify customers, determine their requirements and their expectations.

eselling®

Hopefully you deliver and you'll be called for a repeat order. At this level, there isn't a lot of interaction because the customer only views you as the liaison for the transaction and little else.

People don't like to be sold to – even though they love to buy – and at this lowest level of the relationship hierarchy, the expectation is that you're simply looking for the next opportunity to make a pitch.

In this position, as customer satisfaction increases, your relationship improves.

Value-added Supplier

As your interactions continue, you meet the requirements for the customer and you exceed them as well.

You start to add value to their business.

Through this, your personal relationship with the customer begins to transcend from one of being merely transactional and a proper business relationship starts to emerge.

Solution Provider

As you continue to make a habit of meeting customer needs, you also use your online intelligence skills to monitor the landscape for your customer and your market.

Seeing where trends may match up gives you the ability to anticipate the needs of your customer and advise them as an inside consultant.

Trusted Advisor

As a trusted advisor, you're at the top of the heap.

As a sales professional, this is the ideal position because you're attracting people to you instead of living the constant life of having to make cold calls and beat the pavement for business.

Clients are likely to call you for advice on multiple subjects because you've developed a relationship of trust.

You're recognised as a professional but not one that jumps on a sale at the first smell of blood.

It's Your Business To Be Credible

There's a saying that you're remembered more for what you do than what you say.

This is a corner stone of establishing credibility as well.

Credibility is an expression of your personal brand.

As people are exposed to you, they see how you carry yourself and what you're all about.

In video or audio, you project a certain aura. In more practical terms, we are neurologically programmed to see and hear a myriad cues and signals from facial expressions, body language and vocal patterns. This gives people that feeling that you've no doubt had when meeting someone.

To put your best self forward online, seek to be transparent and authentic in all that you do.

If you're doing some videos and feel nervous in front of the camera, say so.

Use notes if you must and instead of trying to hide them, tell the camera that because you don't want to miss a single point, you're "blatantly" referring to your notes. By claiming ownership of something that might be considered a shortcoming, you gain great credibility by having the courage to call it out.

Another factor that impacts credibility is in how you manage your own communication style.

Different people communicate in different ways. Some are very "bottom line" oriented while others speak in terms of stories. There are people who are very specific when it comes to facts and figures while others are more interested in the general picture.

There is no "right or wrong" in any of these communications styles. Recognise what your natural tendencies are and also that not everyone who reads, watches or listens to your material shares your style. If you tend to round off figures, qualify that when you share something. If you tend to leave out the middle of stories because you're more interested in getting to "the point" then qualify that too. Help others understand where you're coming from so you're not misunderstood in your intentions and you'll even find credibility with people who express themselves very differently.

Credibility extends into how you manage errors and oversights as well as your success. Mistakes happen. It's unrealistic, foolhardy and arrogant to assume they won't. They should be rare, but when they do occur your character is likely to be seen under a brighter light as the issue is managed.

Questions To Help Identify Your Personal Brand

As mentioned, your personal brand comes from within.

It is conveyed through what you do and how others experience you through their interactions with you.

Use the spaces below to write in your roles, styles and skills.

This is where it all starts.

This information is the foundation for any personal brand.

Keep this information handy and refine it as you become more aware of some of the more subtle ingredients in your personal brand.

What is your role?

_____

_____

_____

What is your style going to be?

_____

_____

_____

What key skills can you bring to the table?

_____

_____

_____

After you've worked through these basic questions, you can further develop your personal brand by answering these questions.

Remember, the answers to these questions aren't your brand. They are how your brand "shows up" in the world.

As you reflect on these questions, you may rediscover some things about yourself.

What path led you to the business you're in?

_____

_____

_____

What do you have a knack for?

_____

_____

_____

What's the one thing you're best at solving for yourself or clients?

_____

_____

_____

Who have you worked with in the past? How has that experience shaped you?

_____

_____

_____

What are you most passionate about?

_____

_____

_____

What are your favourite leisure time activities?

_____

_____

_____

How long have you been doing what you do?

_____

_____

_____

What charities are you passionate about?

_____
_____
_____

Why would someone not want to work with you?

_____
_____
_____

How do you want to be remembered?

_____
_____
_____

Alfred Nobel is known today for the Nobel Prize, but he wasn't known that way during his own lifetime. Driven by a desire to invent and explore the fields of science, Nobel is the inventor of dynamite. It was used to shape the very landscape and allow railroad tracks to be run through mountains. It made mining possible in areas where resources were thought to be unattainable.

Unfortunately, dynamite was also used to kill.

While he was still alive, a newspaper ran Nobel's obituary and referred to him as the "merchant of death". Nobel was aghast at the thought of being remembered this way and used his considerable fortune to promote continued innovations in research for years to come with a series of prizes.

Upon study of Alfred Nobel's biography, the passions that fuelled his inventions and the foundation behind the Nobel Prize appear to be one and the same.

Perhaps the creation of the prize was done so as a reaction to the negativity of the obituary text, but the expression of his passion for discovery is no less evident in this than in his earlier achievement.

Creating And Maintaining A Tribe

"The future of marketing is leadership" – Seth Godin

The marketing term "tribe" was coined by best-selling author Seth Godin. It refers to a group of people joined together based on common ideas and ideals.

As people find you online, some will choose to follow what you do.

This may be as a connection on one or more of the social media services or it may be as a subscriber to your email list.

Think of followers as people who have raised their hand to say that they would like to hear more from you. Followers are not always the decision makers but they are people who can participate in the growing of your sphere of influence.

In the past, the way to create power and a following was through the most efficient production. Then it was the biggest media budget. That was followed by the cheapest distribution model or the cheapest labour. According to the popular theory of tribes, we've returned to an element that pre-dates all of that where the new model for change is leadership.

Tribes are created by leadership and led and connected by ideas. Members are not recruited like a group of employees, but are rather attracted to action. By definition, tribes are formed around a very specific idea or challenge to the status quo. Because of this, not everything is suited for a tribe. In Seth's words, if you have a commodity-based, price-drive business, you may not have the makings of a tribe.

SEAN MCPHEAT

Tribes Are Driven By A Challenge

If you sell print on demand technology for creating books at the touch of a button, you challenge the notion that being published requires the backing of a major publisher with the money to print many books to an economy of scale and absorb the costs of extra inventory generated by the process.

So why not bring together people that fit that model? They aren't the big name authors but rather the many who are creating books that appeal to their own tribes.

In one example, shared by Godin in a video interview, there is a coffee shop in London which has created a strong following based around a tribe. Some coffee shops use a reward card as a form of encouraging repeat business and customer loyalty. The owner of this shop does something a bit different. Providing a list of eight competitors, he encourages patrons to visit the competition. They receive a free coffee after completing the list.

Only a dedicated coffee gourmand is likely to do something like this!

It sends a message that the shop owner is very serious about the quality of his product and his actions attract other such enthusiasts to him and his business.

In a world that seems to be driven by safe coffee varieties, the status quo challenged here is the notion that only the super conglomerates can run a successful coffee business today.

While this approach may not scale to be effective – or even possible – for a worldwide coffee business, it can create a powerful and dedicated following for a local business and can certainly work over the Internet as well.

Tribes Are Driven By A Culture

Tribes are driven by the distinction between those on the inside and those on the outside. Again, this means that a commodity-based product is difficult to build a tribe around. In order for there to be a sense of feeling on the inside there must be outsiders too.

Let's say you sell software for managing a paperless office.

You may build a tribe around the environmental benefits of never using paper.

Not all businesses feel motivated for "green" reasons and will not be a part of this circle. This also means that you are able to communicate even more effectively to the people who are on the inside. They're connected by a common idea of how an office should be run.

Wikipedia is an online encyclopedia which boasts millions of articles created by only a few thousand people. There is no manager for wikipedia contributors. They are managed by each other. Mistakes are fixed in hours, instead of the years required by a major encyclopedia. The tools for creating or editing an article on wikipedia are confusing to use for most people. That in itself promotes the tribe because the most prolific contributors have managed to figure it all out. It's almost like a secret handshake.

Tribes Are Driven By Connection

Another characteristic of a strong tribe is the interconnection. Tribes are interlinked and that's what draws people to them. People are drawn to political parties, networking groups, so-called secret societies and even individual web- sites because of the people they can potentially interact with. They are able to feed off each other, taking new ideas to new levels. In the context of your business, these are the people using your products. Their usage exceeds the predictions of anyone in your company as to what to do with your solutions. Your customers are effectively the ground troops and they are far more aware of what to do with your solutions than your company because they're the ones putting your products to real use.

Those who use Twitter most successfully not only engage others through the service but also connect other people together. The best face-to-face networkers do the same thing, regularly introducing people to each other based on common affinity. Tribes exist to exist beyond your control. Strong tribal leaders allow their message to grow beyond them.

Tribes Are Driven By Charisma

You don't need charisma in order to be a leader, but you will have it by virtue of being a leader. Charisma will naturally follow your actions. Steve Jobs and Bill Gates each lead a tribe. Do the differences between a Mac and a PC really make that much difference when it comes to using them as tools with which to do your work? Many people believe they do though they probably can't articulate a single material difference that illustrates why. The mannerisms of these two industry giants are very different and the people in their tribes follow them with the attention more typically associated with rock stars and royalty.

Don't worry if you feel that you lack the personality of a leader. Focus on the ideas that will pull your tribe together and focus on that. Your mission is to find the "true believers" and feed their passions.

Tribes Are Driven By Commitment

You can't create a tribe based on the ideas of a raw food vegan diet and then go back to eating steaks. Tribal authority requires commitment and it requires consistent devotion. You don't need to get everyone to organise themselves around your ideas and form into your tribe. Focus on those who are a part of what you do.

Tribes are not about any technology. They can be created without any Internet tools or social media sites. It is important to understand this before you consider how you might go about building a tribe. With the Internet, it's easier than ever to bring together people and rally around an idea. No one has to worry about driving to a meeting location or whether or not there are enough people in your area to support a tribe. Tribes don't require millions of people. They can operate on dozens.

On The Internet Followers Can Be Fickle!

Because of this it is important to have a strategy for regular content generation.

When somebody joins your mailing list, they should hear from you regularly.

They should also continue to receive information that is to their benefit. One of the chief mistakes made by sales professionals is to launch into a sales pitch too soon. Even though people look online for reasons to trust a person, there is an inherent level of distrust associated with the online world and with sales and marketing professionals in general. eselling® counters this by constantly feeding useful content to build on that trust like deposits into a bank account.

Followers: It's Not (Always) About The Numbers

When social media was first getting attention from the media and the public, it seemed that the only metric worth mentioning was the number of followers you had.

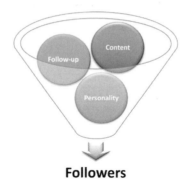

Followers

In the early days of social media sites like Twitter, Facebook and YouTube, the focus was on the number of followers.

While this number still carries weight in some circles, it is not always a clear route to results. If you have 1,000,000 followers on Twitter, it doesn't actually do you any good unless they're the right followers and unless they're paying attention to what you have to say.

There is no way to put a simple monetary value on a follower or a fan.

As much as you may want to put a value on your followers, or be pressured to do so, a follower could be valued at £1,000,000 or £0. This is because there are many valuables which make the determination difficult at best.

Here are just a few examples.

• What is the cost of your item?

• How was the fan or follower acquired?

• What is the relationship between the fan and your product or company?

• How do you interact with or engage your fans?

This conundrum applies to all forms of "followers", from Facebook fans to email list recipients.

I met a business owner once with a mailing list of 20,000 subscribed members.

After building this list he sent a promotional message for a product that was related to the interests of the people on the list. Out of 20,000 people one might expect at least a few sales to be generated by a message that's even poorly written.

He didn't even get a single sale!

This story does have a happy ending!

After this botched sales attempt he began to regularly send messages to the list and he built a relationship with the readers over time.

Sometimes he would forward excerpts from interesting articles, share his own thoughts, and sometimes he asked direct questions of the reader with an invitation to hit reply and send feedback.

In doing so he built a relationship with his list.

He got to know what his followers were looking for. They got used to hearing from him and were reminded of the value they perceived when joining the list in the first place!

The next time he sent a promotional email greater trusted had been established.

There was no need to engage in a lengthy sales pitch. He simply let his followers know that there was something available that he thought was a good fit for them and that it would help them.

SEAN MCPHEAT

I do not recall the exact numbers for the response that he received but he did say that he made well over £10,000 just from a single email out to his list.

Remember, the value is not in your list. It's in the relationship that you have with your list.

How often you engage with your followers is as important as how you engage them. Remember that every person reviewing your content is a real person. They are not bronze statues. They have lives outside of work. They have their own challenges, goals and aspirations.

You may not need 20,000 people on your email list to have the same kind of results. Whether you have a dozen people on your list or 10,000,000, the way that you speak to your reader is the same. You speak directly to the reader.

This model applies to other forms of content online as well. Think of it as though you're sitting in a coffee shop speaking to a friend. While your online content may reflect how skilled, talented, insightful and generally great you are, it's not about that. Your content should be all about your target reader's needs.

When you create video content, or share information through the other venues, solicit feedback and ask questions.

One of the major changes that is shaping the landscape of interaction between people on the Internet today derives from the fact that people are no longer passive content consumers!

Instead, they want to interact, join in and to have their thoughts and feelings known. So good or bad, encourage that kind of interaction with your audience online and it will lead directly to enhanced trust and a better relationship.

Building an active network takes effort. You need to engage.

Building The Tribe

The ultimate aim of any eselling® campaign is to provide great content on an ongoing basis to all of your prospects and clients.

This can be best achieved if you can add them onto an email list and, via an autoresponder, you can communicate regularly with them.

So if it's possible, you need to be offering "an ethical bribe" in return for your viewers email address.

This "bribe" can be in the form of a free whitepaper, for example, or a DVD, a pdf report, or access to some unknown research that will help them.

In order to capture your visitor's email address you'll need to add some code to your web page or blog (this is very easy to do).

You'll then hook this form up to an autoresponder such as:

Get Response – http://www.getresponse.com

1ShoppingCart – http://www.1shoppingcart.com

The fees per month range from $25–$99. All you need to do is add content to the responder and on set dates your list will receive the content!

So you could write 10 newsletters in one day, load them up to the autoresponder and sequence them to be delivered one every 7 days.

Your list will then receive each respective newsletter from you after 7,

14, 21, 28 days etc. for the next 70 days while you can focus on filling the funnel!

Your CRM system may have this functionality so be sure to check it out.

In order to build a strong and loyal tribe you need to regularly be on contact with them with great content. Not sending them some kind of sales message every month but really good content that helps them, surprises them even and makes you stand out.

This is also an example of putting your prospecting on automatic pilot.

Where else could you ever get to "talk" to your funnel once a month without really getting on their nerves!

Embedding Your Brand

Embedding your brand: just what does that mean?

What you have to offer is the single most important aspect of your personal brand, but you need to give it a vehicle in order for anyone to encounter and interact with it – and with you.

In order to embed your brand into anything, you must create something.

On the Internet, this is all about creating content. Doing so is really no different to presenting at association meetings, networking, and following up – or dropping in on – your prospects and clients. These are all things that you've done in the past without the Internet. However, times have changed so you need to update where you're doing these things.

As we've seen in previous examples, there are plenty of options for creating content into which you can embed your brand.

A word of caution: your brand is on display everywhere.

Don't think that just because you're only using Facebook for "personal use" that people aren't looking at your Facebook updates and activities. They are and they are making judgements about who you are based on what they find. It doesn't take much effort to find stories in the news about people who have lost their jobs, been passed over for promotion or weren't hired at all because of their online activities.

Your prospects and clients can make similar assumptions about doing business with you based upon what they find on the Internet.

SEAN MCPHEAT

Perhaps you think that your market isn't technical enough for people to be searching for you online. This is a foolish assumption. Current estimates are that nearly 2 billion people are now actively online. Facebook has over 500 million users who managed to figure out how to get onto their service. LinkedIn has over 100 million users networking through their online service. The maths is simply not on your side to assume that your clients lack the technical skills to search for you through Google.

So continue to build your own content, with your own name in it. Add to the wealth of search results provided by Google when someone searches for you. Yes, they may even find something negative about you that someone else has written about you. Assuming the information is accurate, any attempt to have it removed or "silenced" represents the lowest form of unethical behaviour. Seek instead to build the positive side of your brand by showing people who you are, what you do and how you do it.

Some people have even gone so far as to declare the problems they've had in the past – like a bankruptcy, lost job, failed business – through their own website!

Why wait for someone else to try to post a "scoop" on you when you can probably defuse the situation by simply putting it "out there". Once you do that, it's rather difficult for anyone else to sensationalise it.

Even though we seem to live in a culture that believes you're supposed to present a facade of perfection and never admit to anyone else that you've ever made any mistakes, it's hard for any rational person to believe that such a person actually exists!

It should be even harder to believe that just because your mistakes haven't been presented online, your prospects and clients think you're perfect.

Take the road of authenticity and simply be real.

Generating buzz online is not something that can be described with a recipe-like formula. If it was really that easy, everyone would be doing it.

People form into what author Seth Godin calls a tribe because of common ideas and ideals which they have in common. Tribes are not managed and they do not form just because you snap your fingers and say so.

The closest analogy to all of this is the often misused term "getting your ducks in a row". Many people think this means you get all your details in order, do your preparation work, recruit a team and then at the very end of the process you start leading them. When studying the literal example of this phrase, it's easy to see how absolutely wrong people get it. There's a mother duck and ducklings. The mother duck begins to walk and the ducklings get in a row.

Getting your ducks in a row requires movement on your part. You need to take the first step and head somewhere.

Building your presence online, and injecting your brand into it, follows the real-world example of getting your ducks in a row. You need to start moving somewhere.

Create content. Use Twitter. Prospect on LinkedIn. Create a YouTube video. Write a blog post. And if you do it badly then just learn from it and move on.

It's the simple equivalent of a duck heading in the wrong way and then just changing its direction.

To build buzz and embed your brand into it, focus on solutions.

The reality is that no one cares about your products or your services.

SEAN MCPHEAT

They only care about what they can do. If the web site WillItBlend.com was devoted to talking about the blender, it would be unlikely to generate even the slightest amount of interest with anyone.

But by focusing on what can be accomplished – and with a good dose of humour – this site has made a real name for this commercial blender and a level of viral sharing that is the envy of many marketers.

Here's a quick recap of some of the types of content where you can embed your brand.

Embed Your Brand With Discussion And Forum Groups

Use the search methods discussed earlier to find online hangouts for the types of people who are buying your products and services. Don't jump into a discussion forum with a sales pitch. Engage with them as another interested party. This doesn't mean you hide your true identity and pretend you're just another customer hanging out at the water cooler. That form of spamming is easy to spot by others and the backlash can be significant because it can erode trust in your entire company.

Add value by answering questions and joining in conversations. Be a part of the conversation and share your expertise, knowledge and experience. Building your brand is a long-term strategy. This – like all brand-building approaches – is about creating a presence for yourself.

Embed Your Brand With LinkedIn, Facebook, Twitter And Other Status Updates

People don't want to know what you just had for lunch!

Instead, you need to give value to them in some way or another.

eselling®

Share what's going on with you and your business. When you're testing a new product, say so. When you're getting ready to launch a big promotion, you don't have to create some elaborate system of updates to impress others with how big it is. Just says what's going on.

Far too many people treat social media like a moon launch, while the most successful treat is as a comfortable way to share and engage others.

This is very similar to observing different types of people in other social and networking environments. Those who simply relax seem to be the ones finding the opportunities. There's a lesson to be learned there.

Embed Your Brand In The Groups

Remember to create your own discussions and contribute to the discussions on LinkedIn groups and other groups on the Internet.

This is a great opportunity to prove your worth and to really stand out from everyone else.

The purpose of contributing to these groups is to get you onto the radar of the prospects that you want to attract and also to build up your persona within these groups.

Getting involved in LinkedIn groups will play an important role if you're going to prospect using LinkedIn, but you need to take action and get involved to make it all happen.

Embed Your Brand With Your Blog

A blog may seem to some like nothing more than a diary. In some ways that may be true but, more importantly, it's a venue for you to tell your story. Position yourself as a thought leader by putting that story into the context of what you do. Relate your own personal experiences to what you do. Show others how the world – and your industry – looks through your eyes. Anyone can go to a site like Wikipedia and get data and information on a subject. What they can't get is that information through the lens of your experience.

There's a big difference between telling a person a story and telling them about your product. Even if the story is about the product, the way people tend to experience that approach is far more positive than anything which sounds like a sales pitch. What stories can you tell about your product, your company and your experience in this industry? How has it changed? What have you seen people do? Is there some interesting history that ties to the creating of your product, or your entire industry?

At the end of each blog post, ask the reader a question. Invite them to leave a comment and engage you. For many blogs, you may not have a lot of interaction at first, but stick to it and promote every blog post you write.

Embed Your Brand With Video

Similar to a blog, video gives you the ability to show people who you are, what you do and how you do it through a more engaging medium. If you have a product that can be demonstrated, show everything you can. How can you take a product demonstration to the next level? Can you show it being built? Can you show it being taken apart? Imagine a video that shows a printer stripped down to its screws and reassembled on camera. This is the type of content that is engaging to the viewer. It gives them the feeling of behind-the-scenes access that they wouldn't normally get.

Another great form of video content is to sit with a colleague or a client and talk to them on camera about what they do and how they do it. Don't treat this like a cheap informercial. Think of it as a case study or another form of behind-the-scenes access for the viewer.

YouTube has a limit of 15 minutes per video, which is probably too long for most content anyway. An hour's worth of raw footage could easily be chopped up into 6 to 8 videos. Break the content into bite-sized chunks. That gives you more video titles to share and to get found through the search engines. It also makes viewing your content easier and more convenient.

Video editing is a vast subject and well beyond the scope of this book. If you're spending your time editing videos, you're not doing the real work that brings in sales for you and your company. Outsource, and let an expert do the work for you.

Embed Your Brand By Following Up

When someone visits your main website, your blog, your Facebook fan page or your personal branded company web page you should be getting them on your automated email list so you can follow-up with them over time. Simply saying "join my mailing list" is rarely good enough to get people to join you. Instead, offer them something like a report on how to get the best deals on products in your market, or an index of DIY videos showing the reader how to solve critical problems they're likely to be experiencing.

The bottom line is to offer your target follower something they will value. That means something that will make their life easier by solving one of their problems.

You don't want to be sending these messages out one by one!

Instead, you can use what is known as an autoresponder or an automated email marketing system. There are many of these services available. Instead of having your IT department install a service, I recommend using a third party service to manage your lists because these companies specialise in the kinds of features you need to get the most out of your list.

They are in the business of getting their email messages delivered. Even though people are asking to join your list, some will mark your message as spam at some point.

If enough of them do this, your messages might stop getting delivered to the people who still want to hear from you. By working with an email delivery professional like aweber.com, you can focus your business on what your business should be doing and let someone else worry about the hassle of email delivery issues.

These are a few of the main examples of how you can embed your brand through content. Others include writing reports, sharing pictures and presentations and more. Don't obsess with trying to do it all. Instead, pick a small assortment and master them. As you get comfortable with what you're doing, add something new. Remember that what you're doing relies on tools made possible by the Internet, but what you're doing is very much the same as the activities of top sales and marketing professionals from decades past.

Rinse, Wash & Repeat

"Whatever gets scheduled, gets done!"

Implementing eselling® in an erratic way will not get you the desired results that you're after.

Instead, you need to implement a "Rinse, wash & repeat" system where your content gets done, your prospecting is scheduled and when a new prospect is identified, you know exactly what you are going to do with that prospect.

To implement eselling® you may have to break some of the norms in your organisation.

Many businesses still operate on a 20th century model that insists on a separation between sales, marketing and public relations.

Because eselling® is effectively an amalgamation of all three you'll probably need to seek buy-in from your company.

If that's the case then get it done upfront.

Who is responsible for the content?

Who is responsible for standards?

What can and can't you write about?

Who will do the research?

No two companies implement eselling® in exactly the same way due to the complex nature of organisations.

You need to go over the content contained within this book and produce your own eselling® operating model.

You may want to propose starting your eselling® venture as a pilot project for the company.

When doing so, keep in mind where eselling® fits. You are the sales professional and it is your job to bring in the deals. The purpose of eselling® is to effectively position you online where people are looking for you, and for you to be able to prospect online without having to make hundreds of cold calls each month.

By itself eselling® is not going to do your job for you.

It's about using modern tools that connect you to an audience that no longer responds to traditional forms of sales, marketing and public relations.

Priming The Pump

To get started with the eselling® process, you first need some basic preparation.

Take an inventory and be clear about your unique selling points and the benefits of the products and services that you're selling. You should have this information in mind already, but clarity and focus goes a long way when it comes to an effective eselling® approach.

Make a complete list of all the products and services at your disposal. What markets do these serve? What markets do you want to attract? Be specific. Use this information when you're filling in profiles for social media accounts or bio pages. Identify who it is that you help and what you help them with.

- ✓ Who are you?

- ✓ What do you have?

- ✓ What markets do you serve?

Your Customer Profile

There's an old saying in sales and marketing: If you try to sell to everyone, you'll sell to no one.

No matter how universal your product happens to be, people want to feel as though you're connecting with them.

Before you write a blog post, an article, or shoot any type of video, consider the person at the other end. Notice that I didn't say your audience. I'm not talking about a broad demographic. Who is the person reading your words or listening to you speak?

Even in the world of B2B sales, it is a person that conducts research, shows up at meetings, reviews your products, approves and purchases them and writes a cheque. Each of those people is a real person with a unique background, hopes and dreams. Just like the path in life that led you to where you are, they have walked their own path.

Imagine now a face of one of these individuals at the other end of the Internet connection. What does he or she do? How old are they? What kind of background do they have? What do they like to do outside of work? Build an imaginary file of these people and refer to them when you're creating content. Imagine that a blog post is in fact an email to that specific person. It will have an impact on the style of your writing and even the "energy" you send out through your communications. People respond to this energy and it's the basis of the connection they will feel with you when reading what you have written.

Who Else Is Out There?

Using simple tools like Google, find out who else is selling what you have.

Sometimes they will be direct competition. Other times, you'll find similar products aimed at an entirely different market. How are they positioned? Are they being talked about in the forums and social media sites? What kind of footprint do they leave online?

Using the online intelligence tactics outlined earlier is a great way to keep up with what's being said about you. It's also a great way to monitor the competition.

Create alerts for other products. Someone that isn't direct competition today may be tomorrow. By paying attention to the playing field, you're less likely to be caught unawares.

If you think you don't have any competition, you're probably not looking hard enough. If your market has any worth at all then there are other vendors out there, selling in your space. There may also be vendors selling alternatives to your solution in your space. If another product is masking the need for your products, then it's competition.

Using Google searches, make a note of blogs, social media sites, and forums that are dedicated around your market or industry. Just because they exist doesn't mean they have activity. The only way to tell is by looking at the content and checking dates when possible. Many blogs and forums are virtual ghost towns where the newest content is over a year old. Make a note of these sites, but don't worry about monitoring them too regularly.

Next, use the file type Google search to collect documents created by your competition or other thought leaders in the field. You'll be amazed how many PowerPoint and PDF files you can find in a few minutes. Save them to a folder on your computer. You can't guarantee that they won't be deleted in the future so retain your own library. I've even found price lists and customer presentations through such searches. The information is valuable and easily found.

Do searches through LinkedIn, YouTube, Facebook and Twitter to find more content shared by your competitors. Perhaps another company is providing a free online workshop about how to use their product? Simple keyword searches should turn up such information. After all, they want to be found too.

Create Your Brand

Your personal brand is who you are, but if you're like most people you may not have given a lot of thought to that. Before you start writing blog posts, recording videos or engaging others through LinkedIn, Facebook or Twitter, give some thought to how to want to "show up" online. Emotion is always muted through online interaction so the goal isn't to "adopt" a false persona – unless you're truly fabricating a fictional character like the Old Spice guy.Instead aim to emphasise the qualities you want to put on display to the public.

Increase Your Internet Footprint

The easiest way to get started with eselling® is by picking one form of content and engagement and working with it until you feel comfortable. Then add something else to the mix. For most people a blog is a good place to start. Aim to write something every single day. It doesn't have to be long. Use the keyword research to figure out questions and answer them with how to articles and shared thoughts and visions.

SEAN MCPHEAT

As you build your own blog presence, monitor other blogs from thought leaders in your field. Leave thoughtful comments for blog posts. Become known for your own insight as a contributor to what's happening in your part of the world. Don't assume you're the only person out there.

When you feel that you have a handle on the pulse of the market, approach other blog owners and submit guest blog content. This is one of the best ways to generate traffic and followers for your own blog. Having a guest post on another popular blog is seen as an endorsement. People will notice and they will follow you through your online presence as you become known.

Add other forms of content as you get the hang of what you've started with, but don't feel that you have to. There is no rule that says you must be a part of every conversation. It's not possible anyway. It's far better to have a rock solid blog and no video content than to be weak in both areas because you spread yourself too thin.

Promote Yourself And What You Create

Don't forget to engage your prospects, your clients and even your friends when it comes to your newly created online presence. If you create a Facebook page, ask people you know to "like it". Don't take on the fallacious assumption that if you build it, they will come.

That never works.

Take steps to promote your new content to get some momentum. Ask people you know to comment on your blog posts or answer your polls. To others, this establishes "social proof" and encourages others to comment and interact too.

As you establish yourself online, seek out magazines and other media outlets.

eselling®

Just like bloggers, these people are looking for content too. Having a magazine run one of your articles can be a real boost to your online positioning. It's similar to the "As Seen On TV" logo some products carry. It doesn't matter if it was seen on TV at three in the morning, it was seen and that alone gets the attention of many on an emotional level.

The Journey Of A 1,000 Steps

To be effective in eselling® you need to be both methodical and consistent.

If you decide to start with blogging as your first step in building your online presence then be consistent. Sporadically posting to your blog is not effective and will not get the job done. The same holds true for any type of online content creation.

Old content will always benefit you as it remains in the search engines to be found by new people. However, an effective online presence is one that is also fresh. Relying solely on the benefits of old content is not an effective strategy and can even create confusion among those who follow you as they wonder if you're still in business.

What Now?

This book has shown you the model for eselling® and all of its component parts.

It's shown you how to position yourself online and how to get found more often. It's shown you how to build trust with people who discover you and it's shown you how to prospect online using social media.

Each of the components themselves would merit a whole book to themselves!

SEAN MCPHEAT

What you now need to do is to create your own company version of eselling®.

How will it work for you?

What components will be in your eselling® model on day 1, day 60, day 90?

Who will be involved to make it happen?

Who will monitor standards?

How can you schedule eselling® into your ways or working?

Remember that your initial blog posts, articles or videos may not be perfect.

Don't worry about it.

Doing them is a part of the process. Not doing them only ensures you'll never get better. Simply pay attention to what you're doing and seek to improve constantly.

We're in a world where the Internet is becoming more and more important to all of us in some way or another. It's time to embrace this and to start making your move.

One thing is for certain; the Internet and its usage is only going to get more popular so it's better to be "in" now rather than later on down the line.

It's time for you to use the Internet to your advantage and for you to use it as your prospecting, branding and ultimately, your sales vehicle. Remember, you'll only succeed by taking action so don't let this book just gather dust on your shelf at home.

eselling®

Instead, keep referring to it, make notes on it and above all else act upon it.

That's the real path to victory.

I wish you all the very best

Sean McPheat

"If you want to increase your rate of success, double your rate of failure." – **Tom Watson, Founder, IBM**

eselling®

Open & In-House Training Courses

We hope that this book has given you a great insight into the eselling® approach.

If you'd like to take it one step further, we run a number of eselling® **open courses** at various locations throughout the country or you can have your sales team trained in the eselling® approach as an **in-house training programme**.

As an in-house programme we will tailor and produce your very own eselling® model that suits the way that you sell and how your company is set up.

Please visit the following websites for further details:

www.e-selling.com

www.mtdsalestraining.com

SEAN MCPHEAT

eselling®

Become Licensed To Deliver eselling® Training

If you are a trainer then you can become licensed in the eselling® approach and you can then deliver the training to your own clients. You'll attend a train-the-trainer masterclass in the eselling® approach, receive all of the trainer notes, powerpoints, materials etc. and you'll also cover how to tailor the model for your own in-house clients.

Please visit the following website for further details:

www.e-selling.com

About The Author

Sean McPheat

Sean McPheat is a recognised thought leader in the areas of:

- Selling and Sales Management

- Internet Marketing

- Entrepreneurialism

Founder and MD of international sales training firm MTD Sales Training, Sean and his team of sales trainers have delivered training to over 1500 different organisations from around the world.

Sean has been featured on CNN International, the BBC, ITV, The Guardian, Arena Magazine, Marketing Weekly, The Hong Kong HR Journal and radio stations such as BBC WM, Insight Radio and LBC (London's Big Conversation) and he has over 250 other media credits to his name.

Having built MTD Training from a bank balance of zero, he's living proof that with hard work and the right strategy, anything is possible!

Sean's weekly email tips go out to over 60,000 people interested in sales and management and he's a big player in the Internet marketing scene.

Sean is a much sought after motivational speaker on all topics relating to sales, business improvement and entrepreneurialism. Some of his highly acclaimed keynote speeches include:

"Confessions Of A Rock Star Sales Person", "Confessions Of A Serial Closer", "The 9 Deadly Sales Mistakes & How To Avoid Them", "How To Turn Sales Talent Into Sales Performance", "Smile & Dial R.I.P", "Loyal Customers? You Gotta Be Kidding Me!", "Using The Internet To Prospect".

Sean has also delivered many other keynote topics around the exact requirements of the audience who always go away informed, motivated and entertained.

You can email Sean directly at: sean.mcpheat@mtdsalestraining.com
Sean does respond to every email he receives.

Useful Resources

Need Some Sales Training?

MTD Sales Training have delivered sales training to over 1500 different organisations. MTD offer both **in-house** and **open training** courses including consultative selling, cold calling, eselling®, negotiation skills, sales management, sales presentation skills, coaching skills, advanced sales, sales for beginners and many more.

Visit: www.mtdsalestraining.com

Want Sean To Speak At Your Event?

Sean will inform, ignite and motivate your audience. His style is direct, thought provoking, challenging and fun! To enquire about Sean's availability:

Visit: www.seanmcpheat.com

Receive Sean's Email Sales Tips

Sean will send you a practical sales tip each week so you keep sharp and focused on the job in hand!

Visit: www.emailsalestips.com

Sean's Sales Blog Full Of Tips And Insights

There are hundreds of articles and tips at Sean's blog. Sean updates the blog a couple of times each week with new thoughts, approaches and knowledge

Visit: www.mtdsalesblog.com

Follow Sean On Twitter

Follow Sean's tweets and musings

Visit: www.twitter.com/seanmcpheat

ALSO BY SEAN McPHEAT

Drive Time Sales Strategies

39 Practical "HOW TO" Sales Tips
While You're On The Way To The Sale

In this 5 CD sales programme, Sean McPheat covers some of the most up to date and effective sales techniques to readdress the balance of power with the modern day buyer. Specifically designed for you to listen to in your car or when you're on the move, Sean will become your very own sales coach out on the road with you!

Topics such as planning, preparation, cold calling, objection handling, closing, economy excuses, existing supplier strategies and loads more besides are covered in short, sharp, focused sessions.

"They went in the car this morning and 2 hours later I got to my appointment and won the sale, it was just like you were sitting in the room with me"

"Just By Adopting A Couple Of Suggestions Made By You They Have Both Now Signed 3 Year Contracts And Got 3 Referrals (Total Value Of

SEAN MCPHEAT

Contracts Signed £22,000 Per Annum And Without Any Sort Of Discount Structure!)"

"I use them on a regular basis to prepare for meetings and presentations, to improve my sales skills and to give me motivation when I have a poor meeting or a bad day..."

For Further Details Visit

www.drivetimesales.com